LIGHT, LOVE, HEA

THE FOREST TABERNACLE

Memoir of Catholicism, Jesus, and a Sexual Assault on a Bicycle Tour

Dr. Patrick Milroy

International Health Publishing
www.InternationalHealthPublishing.com

INTERNATIONAL HEALTH PUBLISHING
Established 2008
Publishing Group Affirming Truth & Innate Wisdom

First International Health Publishing trade paperback edition November 2013.

FRIENDLY NOTE: International Health Publishing is committed to publishing literary works of quality and integrity. In this light, we present this book to readers around the world; however, the memoir, the experiences, and the words and opinions are the author's alone. This book is a work of creative nonfiction in the form of a memoir. Events and conversations are portrayed to the best of Patrick Milroy's memory, and we all recognize *that human memory can be deeply flawed.* While all the stories in this book are true, some names and identifying details have been changed to protect the privacy of people and places involved. Everything here is true, but it may not be entirely factual. The author has tried to recreate events, locales and conversations from his memories of them; yet in order to maintain their anonymity, in some instances the names of individuals and places have been changed. Admittedly, the author may have changed identifying characteristics and details such as physical properties, occupations and places of incidence. This book is a combination of facts about Patrick Milroy's journey and certain embellishments. As such, names, dates, places, events, and details are altered, invented, and edited for literary effect. Readers and interpreters should not consider this book anything other than a work of literature.

For information about special discounts for bulk purchase, please write to writer@InternationalHealthPublishing.com.

International Health Publishing can bring authors to your live events.

For more information or to book an event,
contact writer@InternationalHealthPublishing.com or for more information visit us online: www.InternationalHealthPublishing.com
www.TheForestTabernacle.com

The Forest Tabernacle:
Memoir of Catholicism, Jesus, and
a Sexual Assault on a Bicycle Tour
Dr. Patrick Milroy

ISBN-13: 978-0-9857956-6-5
ePUB ISBN-13: 978-0-9857956-7-2
Library of Congress Control Number: 2013951075
SAN 856-6925

Manufactured in the United States of America, and printed on the finest 100% postconsumer-waste recycled paper
10 9 8 7 6 5 4 3 2 1

PRAISE FOR

The Forest Tabernacle

"Beautifully written with such depth and honesty. You'll be carried off on the bike along with Patrick through the joys, the victories and the tortures. Patrick showed amazing character and insight in questioning the domination of the Catholic Church; bringing a new truth to true communion with Jesus, and a sense of deep healing from trauma. A spiritual journey of introspection and religious questioning that all should undertake – without having to ride the thousands of miles."

   ~ Dr. Anne Desneiges D.C., Owner, Inner Waves Centre for
   Well-Being, Halifax, NS

"*The Forest Tabernacle* is a moving and reflective memoir; a frightening story that, despite seemingly insurmountable odds, unfolds into an inspiring, powerful endpoint. During his intense spiritual and physical journey, Dr. Milroy explores themes and questions relevant for us all. His description of his night in the woods – the turning point in his understanding of himself, his relationship with God, his family and religious upbringing – and how he has worked through its aftermath, reminds us of our vulnerability and

assures us that we have the potential to overcome even the darkest moments in our lives."
~ Maria DiDanieli

"A provocative look at one's life-altering journey from tragedy to triumph, Dr. Patrick Milroy's *The Forest Tabernacle* offers a vulnerable and honest account, deeply griping the truth about personal perseverance and endurance that leads to a transformational encounter with the living Christ. Be inspired as history becomes his-story."
~ Rev. Dr. Lennett J. Anderson, *Overseer, EBC: The MEETing Place,* Halifax, NS

"The color of the words on the pages and the profound insights will leave you feeling enriched as you read this inspirational journey of finding God with a bicycle. Great read!"
~ Dr. Dena Churchill, Author of *Divinity in Divorce*

"Does the Roman Catholic Church still matter? Dr. Patrick Milroy grapples with this and other questions of faith. A harrowing night, which begins in his tent, threatens to derail him, but his love of nature and biking win out. *The Forest Tabernacle* is at turns raw, moving, and poetic. A standout read."
~ Voula Kappas-Dunn, Writer Contributor, *Thirteen Ways from Sunday,* and *Grey Area*

"I kept up with your blog after we met and reviewed the previous portions also. The focus on the church marques was really interesting to me. Churches are places of worship and the simple means of a sign says much about them. *Come and worship here,* I would want to believe was the stated or underlying message of each marquee you recorded. Those signs were the first evaluation of the folks inside the four walls. Patrick Milroy also had a sign identifying him; I quickly evaluated what was inside his 'four walls' and realized I wanted to know more. Our brief encounter was exactly like a roadside church marquee – may not know everything about this person but what I can hear and see tells me all is well and I want all the best for my new found friend."

~ Terry M Landreth, www.camdenbikes.com, St. Marys, Georgia

"I heard *"it is not the destination, it is the journey."* For Patrick Milroy, it was both. His words take you back to a time where a young man is in search of his meaning. This story, however blunt, at times, makes you take pause, and is of one man's need to find answers – answers to who he was and of who he has become. His need to retrace his path is one felt by a lot of people and this book may just be the answer to what others may need – to travel along with him and to realize that there is light at the end of a very dark tunnel. His story is one of hope – hope to overcome challenges and obstacles and even though his journey was reliving his past, he gives people the assurance that no matter what the obstacle or the challenge, it is sometimes necessary to find out who you were and why in order to be grateful for who you are today. Each destination, each detour, each roadblock took Patrick to places where he needed answers and these answers brought him some peace which is sometimes what we need in order to move forward. Patrick Milroy is a man of integrity, kindness, love and commitment. He demonstrates courage and has a strength within that makes him able to write this book and to show others that it is not always the journey but the destination."

~ Deborah J. Lohrenz, CIM, RPR, CMP, CCP, CCPT, Profession Life and Career Coach, DJ Lohrenz Consulting & Coaching Inc.

For Sean,
Mom loves you,
Dad loves you,
Jesus loves you.

Contents

Forward

I took little notice of the powder blue KLM luggage tag on the handle of the luggage cart I pulled from the self-serve kiosk in the Toronto airport. I loaded the luggage and walked toward a waiting rental car, fuzzy headed from the fatigue of a busy week at my chiropractic clinic. I had been up nearly the entire night before writing reports, trying to clear my plate, before what I had hoped would be a good weekend away, learning and meeting colleagues at the continuing education seminar being held at my Alma Mater, the Canadian Memorial Chiropractic College. My late flight from Halifax, Nova Scotia had allowed me to care for as many patients as possible on that Friday before leaving.

The airport parking garage was dimly lit as I made my way toward the rental car. I clicked the remote entry button on the car key to see the parking lights of the awaiting vehicle flash confirmation of my successful find. There was a particular darkness at the rear of the vehicle as I loaded the trunk with luggage. The dim lighting and my fatigue contributed to cloudy absentmindedness.

I fiddled with the GPS, finally entering the address of the northeast Toronto hotel where I would spend the next three nights.

At the hotel in Toronto, after a long hot shower, I intended to sit at the room's desk to check e-mail on my laptop. *Where's the laptop case?* I searched the room. *Must have left it in the rental car.* I dressed again, pulled on my shoes without socks and headed into the cold February Toronto night to grab my laptop case from the car. I searched: the trunk, the back seat, the front seat – no laptop case. Walking back into the hotel lobby, I stopped by the front desk thinking maybe I left it sitting on a hotel lobby chair when I checked in. The front desk staff had not seen a laptop.

My mind raced – where could it be? Did I leave it on the plane? No, I recall packing it into its case and carrying it off the plane. My ears prickled as the realization hit: I had left the case on the cart in that dimly lit rental-car parking garage! My heart began to beat faster bearing the gravity of the loss. The case held one of the journals from my 1986 bicycle tour. The laptop held the working manuscript of this book, based upon those journals coupled with my memories.

"Sir, where do you think you left your laptop case?" The woman in the airport security office listened to my explanation as I heard her fingers clicking away on a computer keyboard.

"I think I left it sitting on a luggage cart at the P2 level of the terminal where I picked up my rental car."

"Sir, I'm just reading a report on my screen that says a black case such as the one you describe was found at that location. The bomb squad canine unit was dispatched. The package was declared safe and it will be at the airport security office in the morning."

"You have no idea... thank you! What a relief. Thank you!"

"Okay sir, you can rest easy and pick up your laptop tomorrow morning."

Bomb squad dogs had been dispatched to deal with my laptop case. A black laptop case left unattended in the airport. They take things like that very seriously since 9-11. I'm glad too; otherwise someone may have walked away with it instead of security being called. It goes to show how much they are on their toes. The world had drastically changed since September 11, 2001 when terrorists flew hijacked airplanes into the twin towers of the World Trade Center in New York City and into the Pentagon in Washington, DC.

I crawled into bed admonishing myself for not noticing the case on the cart. *I always get absentminded when I feel stressed.* I fell into light, fitful sleep, recalling my 1986 vision of the towers falling coupled with the terror from the assault I had experienced.

Around the laptop case handle was the powder blue KLM luggage tag and a tag from the canine security service. I recalled that the KLM tag was the same tag as the one attached to the handle of the luggage cart. Why did they put the KLM luggage tag on my laptop case? I unhooked the luggage tag and stared down at the name and address. The address was an Ontario one. The name on the address was unmistakably Islamic. No wonder they called the bomb squad! I turned and looked at the young security attendant and saw her grinning ear to ear. Thank God my laptop was found.

The memoir you are about to read is true. Because key characters in the book are connected to a crime, and have not been brought to justice, some names and places have been changed. I am acutely aware that not everyone would want their name associated with a memoir dealing with religion and sexual assault, therefor other names and places have been changed as well.

I began writing about my 1986 bicycle tour as part of a healing journey. Writing can be healing. Putting words from your memories onto paper has a special cleansing and power, especially when key memories have been repressed for over twenty years, as a part of survival.

THE FOREST TABERNACLE

Memoir of Catholicism, Jesus, and a Sexual Assault on a Bicycle Tour

I
A Balancing Act

⁸ For bodily exercise profits a little, but godliness is profitable for all things, having promise of the life that now is and of that, which is to come.
1 Timothy 4:8 NKJV

Mom watched intently as I loaded and reloaded the panniers of the Norco Monterey SL twelve-speed bicycle. Lines deepened on her brow as she watched me. She sat perched on an iron chair in the screened back porch. Her lips were pursed taut as she gazed at me. At fifty-two years of age, with a crop of grey hair, she had a fresh attractiveness that belied her years of homemaking.

Long periods of silence fell between us and I had become a master at reading the slightest change in her facial expression. This evening's look was a complete soliloquy in disapproval, dissuasion, and worry.

Mom continued to study me, as I got ready for my tour. I was her lanky but athletic six-foot-two inch son. Skin, some of it lightly freckled, was draped over muscle that had been built through hours of basketball play, gym workouts, and miles upon miles of cycling. My eyes were darker than my brown, soft, wavy hair, which would curl from sweat or humidity. Pausing, I combed my fingers through my hair.

"Pat, are you sure you know what you're doing?"

"Yeah, Mom. I'm trying to find the best way to pack these bags so the weight on the bike will balance."

"That's not what I mean, Pat. You're twenty-four, but I still think of you as my little boy. I mean, are you sure you can handle a trip like this?"

"Mom, I have to do this trip."

Money for the tour wasn't an issue. I neither asked my parents for money to take the tour, nor did they give me any. I had worked throughout my university education on jobs ranging from factory materials handler to forklift truck driver at Labatt's Brewery, to work at group homes for the disabled. By the time I was ready to leave on the bicycle tour, I had a twenty-five-hundred-dollar wad of traveler's checks. Most of the traveler's checks were packed in an easily accessible wallet in the front handle bar pack.

Dad made his way onto the sun porch at the rear of their home in St. Thomas, Ontario, where I was packing the bike. "How's it coming, Packer?"

"Good, Dad."

He stood peering at me. Nearly the same age as Mom, he had brown eyes sparkling with boyish charm. Dad removed his golf cap and rubbed his bald head, adjusting the few strands of combed-over hair he still sported.

"I have something for you, Pat," Mom said. She peered up at Dad and then she handed me the two cards she had been holding. The pastel green and purple envelopes matched heavy bond parchment cards within. On the green card was printed, *"Time and caring have made us – FAMILY."* Mom's pretty, sweeping penmanship read, *"We wish you good luck, Pat. Love always – Your Family."* The green card stated, *"There's a time for believing in yourself. That time is now."* Again Mom had written on the card, *"Dear Patrick. Stay happy! Love, Mother and Dad. Have a safe, happy trip."*

"Thanks, Mom." I walked over to her chair and leaned down to hug her, "Thanks for understanding." *She's really afraid for me, but I have to take this trip.*

"Thanks, Dad." We shook hands firmly, looking into each other's eyes, and then gave each other an awkward hug.

"Pat, you make sure you go to Church during this trip. You may not always be able to, but try. If you ever get in trouble, find a Catholic Church and get help."

"Okay, Dad." I wanted to tell him about my struggle with the Roman Catholic faith, but I knew that there was no point. Dad knew I no longer went to Church. His response whenever I had attempted to discuss it was, "I've failed. You're nothing but a bloody heathen. I'll rot in hell because of this." Still, I longed for him to listen, and to understand.

Dad, I understand. You've never questioned your faith. I wish you could understand the fear and confusion I've had in questioning and leaving my faith.

"Let's see how balanced the bike is." I righted it away from the table it was leaning on. I found the balance point and slowly took my hands off it. The bike stood motionless. Mom and I both waited for it to begin tipping to one side or the other, but it stood there in perfect balance, like a ballet dancer holding a difficult pose.

"Pat, that's amazing. I guess you *do* know what you're doing."

"Thanks, Mom." The balancing, loaded-down bicycle gave me a sense of certainty of what I was doing and helped to wash away my pangs of regret over Mom's fear.

I had made my decision to bicycle from St. Thomas, Ontario, to Florida almost two months earlier. Spiritual turmoil had led to the decision to make the *go find your self, young man* journey.

It was time to figure out what I was going to do with my life. I was reading Richard Bach's book, *A Gift of Wings* at the time, and I wrote his words in my journal:

"Time means nothing. Time is just the way we measure the gaps between not knowing something and knowing it, or not doing something and doing it."

I was excited, and deep down I knew cycling to Florida was exactly what I wanted and needed to do. That bicycle was balanced on the eve of my tour, but my life was not.

I was the oldest of six kids. We were all fairly close in age Mom having given birth to all of us within an eight-year time span. Our household was a busy one, with the garage door almost always open. The garage, jammed with bicycles, golf clubs, tools, garden implements, sports equipment, and boxes of stuff that Mom had no idea where to put, was our portal in and out of the house.

I recall at age seventeen, entering the open garage as I arrived home from the YMCA gym. The stock-ends of my two BB guns were protruding from one of the garbage cans. I hadn't touched those guns since our move from Ohio to Ontario the previous year. I pulled the guns out of the can and studied the broke-in-half state that they were both in and knew that my little brothers, Dan and Mark, fourth and fifth in the birth order, had something to do with that state. I felt a loss, loss of something that I had called my own. There wasn't much private in that home. I needed to get the full story.

"Mom, what happened to my guns?" I stood holding them.

"Put those back in the trash where they belong."

"Who did this?"

"I did." Mom was still obviously angered over whatever had transpired.

"I need to know. Why?"

"You can thank your brothers for that. I broke those guns over my knee after I found them doing what they were doing."

"What were they doing?"

"Shooting each other."

Dad had nicknamed Dan and Mark, *Pic* and *Bic* because of their incessant fighting and troublemaking. Pic and Bic lay claim to a series of childhood antics that would make any newscaster green with envy. The BB gun incident was definitely in the top-ten news highlight reel.

You see, Pic and Bic just weren't shooting each other with BBs. They had donned football helmets and ski goggles. Sitting twenty feet from one another in their basement bedroom beds, they had fired finishing nails at each other. Mom had heard the cursing, laughing, and repeated *pop* of the guns. She had walked downstairs to find Pic and Bic pointing at one another. Mark had two finishing nails lodged in the skin over his chest with a trail of blood dripping down. Mom had dealt with the problem.

The span of ages seems greater when you are younger. My sister Callista, we call her Callie, was the next oldest to me. Then came Amy, then Dan and Mark, and finally Sarah. As a kid, I saw Mom and Callie spend a lot of time with young Sarah. That left my sister Amy. I did not consciously realize it, but I think Amy and I naturally gravitated to one another in the busy household because we were both relatively alone in the family.

The next morning Mom and Dad woke early with me. After breakfast I rolled the laden bicycle from the back porch to the front of the house. Having said goodbye the night before, my brothers and sisters were still asleep. Mom and Dad joined me at the front of the house, and our goodbyes were awkward, yet loving.

I coasted the bike down the driveway and onto the street, waving to Mom and Dad, who stood watching me, smiling. I knew Mom was crying. Dad made his attempt to comfort and reassure her by placing his arm around her.

The September eighth, 1986 morning was bright and peaceful, and five degree Celsius crispness heralded the end of summer, but the day warmed by noon. Cycling was easy. Southwestern Ontario's secondary roads were mostly straight and flat as they brought me past mature, lush, green corn, and tobacco fields ready for the fall harvest.

Somewhere just east of Port Burwell, cycling down Road 42, I was hit with a profound sense of freedom. The rhythm of my pedaling legs had been the background to my meditation and prayer time since high school. On this day that rhythm combined with my welcome freedom to bring a chill through my body. Profound clarity. Every fiber of my being sang with joy. *This is it. You're doing exactly what you're supposed to be doing.* The sensation coursing through my mind and body made the pedals feel light.

Mysteriously, silence of the hot afternoon on that empty Southwestern Ontario highway gave way to a chorus of high-pitched buzzing in the air. I could no longer feel the bicycle. I could no longer feel my body. The sensation continued as the road and surrounding farmland swept past me. I felt as if I was flying. My body tingled, and gooseflesh spread over my torso and down my arms and legs. I sensed a cast of angelic presences joining me in celebration of my adventure.

I continued East with a stiff wind at my back, and bright sun on my face from a cloudless sky. The perfection of the day was undeniable: perfect freedom, perfect cycling, complete joy.

The first day ended at Turkey Point Provincial Park. The park's oak and fir trees offered security, peace, and privacy. I leaned my bicycle against the edge of the picnic table as I unpacked my tent and sleeping bag.

Pitching the tent was an automatic task after my numerous bicycle camping trips. During summers, if I had a weekend off work, I would take a long ride on a Saturday, camp at one of Ontario's Provincial Parks, and then ride back on Sunday. Bicycling had been a long-time escape for me.

Once the tent was set up, I walked away from the campsite. My six-foot-two-inch frame had been in the saddle for many hours. Walking around the campsite, I noticed my awkwardness, my leg muscles fatigued from pedaling.

I discovered a playground within the Park. Reaching up to the monkey bars, I lifted my feet from the ground, allowing my spine to stretch out. After a good stretch and a few chin-ups I walked back to the campsite to gather my towel, soap, toothpaste, and toothbrush. I had chosen to pitch my tent not far from the campground's showers. The water beating down on my body cleansed me of dried, salty sweat and reminded me of the day's heavenly celebration of freedom.

I was born in St. Paul, Minnesota, at St. Joseph's Hospital, to parents who attended St. Odelia's Catholic Church, and they had named me after my maternal Irish grandfather who had been named after Ireland's patron, Saint Patrick. Born on the eighth day of the eighth month in the year 1962, I entered the world amongst this quadruple set of Saints, making any future notion of questioning or leaving the Catholic faith as difficult as a black man becoming President of the United States of America.

So here I was on this bicycle tour, questioning the faith that had formed my identity. My intuition was that I would find God in Nature, yet my Church told me it was more important to seek God in the ritual and tradition of the Mass.

I feel closer to God when I'm in the woods, surrounded by His creation. The church feels contrived, false, and empty. Why can there not be a relationship between the Christianity that I grew up with and finding God in nature? Thank God for parks like this one! I stood next to a tall spruce tree, looking up into the high branches.

Trees were happy places for me. My goal had always been to climb higher in the tallest maple tree behind our Chagrin Falls, Ohio, home. On one particular day I had climbed higher than ever before. When I started the climb, I had no particular goal in mind. Climbing trees was my escape, my adventure.

I had risen deftly, assessing each branch for size and strength. *Stay in the middle of the tree. The weight of your body is too great for just one limb. Straddle forks from different branches.*

I had quickly come to the spot in the tree that marked my previous highest attempt. Pausing, I continued to study the branches above. *Figure out the safest, strongest path.* A warm breeze blew gently, causing the leaves to rustle. *Wind is not your friend at this height. Rest here until the wind stills.*

The choices for hand and footholds became fewer the higher I climbed. The tree limbs supporting my eleven-year old body now bent with my weight.

There it was, about three feet above my head: the last and only limb that could safely bear my weight. I felt a nervous quiver through my legs. Like an uncertain groom at the wedding altar, I contemplated the next and last move. Inhaling deeply, I used my arms to hold my body weight as I brought my right leg toward that fork.

Using my right hand, I grabbed a higher branch and pulled my body from its near horizontal position. *Right hand strong, right leg secure.* I reached higher with my left hand. My left leg dangled in mid air. Using both arms, I pulled upward allowing my bent right leg to fully extend. I was looking down at the security of my right foot, when I felt a sensation: warm sunshine now kissed my cheek.

This was my reward. My head was completely above the canopy of the tree. I felt success, elation. I gazed at the sloping canopy and I studied the rooflines of our two-story home some twenty feet below. Looking out further, I saw the rooftops of other homes in our neighborhood. Lake Lucerne, glistening blue, lay like a gem at the end of Westhill Drive. Way off in the distance was the Tanglewood Subdivision and Golf Course.

The wind gently blew again. I swayed in unison with the entire canopy. *Had any other kid in the world ever climbed higher in a tree than I did today?*

Again the wind blew. This time I swayed precariously, which snapped me from my daydream. *Okay, time to come down. Careful.* I contemplated the choices I had made in the ascent, now in reverse. My legs shook nervously as I lowered my body, handhold by handhold, until I was again in midair, my body near horizontal. *Release your right foot. Put your left foot on that limb. Got it. Phew.* I rested. Now I was in familiar territory, and the climb down became easy.

On the last branch, I held on with both hands, allowing my body to stretch, before releasing my grip and landing in the grass below. The ground felt foreign, firm, and without enchantment. I took a celebratory breath, deep and filled with contentment.

Smiling at the thirteen-year old maple tree memory, I turned my attention back to the campsite. I draped my wet towel over the handle bar and cross tube of the bicycle, and sat down at the picnic table to replenish my energy with food and to write in my journal.

July thirty-first was the last time I wrote in my journal. The buzz of preparation and excitement for the tour had made journal writing a low priority, yet journal writing had become my way of navigating life through a quagmire of jumbled emotions, raging hormones, and relationship troubles. I wrote down the day's highlights, and I wrote of my inner turmoil.

A coolness came into the park as the sun dipped into the horizon through the oak and fir trees. I cocooned myself into the tent and sleeping bag. Sleep was deep and welcomed.

II
A Doe

⁹ The voice of the Lord makes the deer give birth,
And strips the forests bare;
And in His temple everyone says, "Glory!"
¹⁰ The Lord sat enthroned at the Flood,
And the Lord sits as King forever.
¹¹ The Lord will give strength to His people;
The Lord will bless His people with peace.
Psalm 29:9-11 NKJV

The sound of my bicycle tires on the pavement was barely audible in the silence and stillness of the early morning. Suddenly, there was movement in front of me. The air became electric, as a big whitetail deer ran across the road only ten feet in front of me. The smoothly paved road was cold and dewy, causing the doe's front hooves to slide. She twisted her head and body for balance with muscles that rippled. She shot a glance at me, and our eyes locked for an instant. I recognized the fear in hers. The bicycle and I were completely foreign to her. Coasting to a stop, I watched the creature regain her footing and then bound off into the thicket. The slight crunch of dry undergrowth grew fainter with her retreat. Standing, I offered a silent wish that her fear of me would be wiped away.

I had the wind at my back, sunshine, and easy terrain, all the way to Niagara Falls, Ontario. Crossing the border into the U.S. the next morning was an important milestone. I phoned home out of obligation rather than to quell any homesickness. Missing home was not even a faint feeling.

I coasted my bike to a stop at the Whirlpool Bridge immigration building. A U.S. Customs officer walked out of the door and confronted me. He cocked his head to one side and squinted.

"Park your bike right here and come into the office."

"Can I lean it on the building? I don't have a kickstand."

"Right there. Nobody will touch it." He motioned to the side of the building with a dismissive wave.

Inside the modest building, an American flag flanked a photograph of President Ronald Reagan. The flag was welcoming to me – this was the country of my birth. I stood at the counter as he walked behind me through a gate to his side of the counter.

"I need to see some ID. Where you going?"

"Florida." I handed him my Ontario driver's license.

"Florida?" He raised both eyebrows and tilted his head back to eye me closely. "Florida, on that?"

"Yeah."

"How old are you?" He looked at my driver's license to check my age.

"Twenty-four. I'm taking the term off university to take this trip."

"There's no drugs or alcohol with you?"

"No, sir."

"No weapons of any type?"

"No, sir."

"You be careful." He handed me back my license.

"I will. Thanks."

Niagara Falls, New York, had a tough, down and out, dreary feel. I kept pedaling to Akron, New York. An occasional drizzle complemented the cloudy, cool day.

As soon as I turned my bicycle southward on Highway 77, I met hills and a stiff headwind. Rolling farmland and woodland offered a visual reward for the hard pedaling. A paved shoulder along Highway 787 gave protection from the traffic.

This is more peaceful. Tough riding, but more peaceful. Keep pedaling. Push through the leg pain. I'm just adjusting to long rides. Hmm, should I stop and camp here in Darien Center? I know there's a campground. Nah, keep going. See what's over the next hill.

The goal of getting to the top of each hill to see the view on the other side kept me pedaling. I cycled to Java Center, probably further than I should have. *Tomorrow morning I'll know by the feel of my legs if it was too much.*

Beaver Meadows Wilderness Family Campground was a rustic place. The campsite was almost empty, but had a charm that made me hope children ran free there during summer days.

The morning of September eleven was stormy, full of powerful wind gusts. Tree limbs blew in unnatural directions to show the underside of leaves. Drizzle became steady rain, which became a torrential downpour. Heavy, low, dark clouds were driven by the warm wind. I huddled in my tent, journaling.

I went for a walk around the campground, which now appeared to be a secluded, romantic hideaway. Energetic frogs leapt through the wet grass. The might of the storm still hung in the air. I found a playground, went for a swing, and daydreamed about the family I would like to take to this campground. No embarrassment entered my mind about being a twenty-four-year old man swinging like a kid. I was feeling as free as the wind, which was still very gusty. The cloud cover finally began to break up. The sun peeked through every once in a while.

Back at the campsite, I readied all my gear for a quick pack in the morning. The campground had a special lure that found me taking another walk. The deep well-water of the park quenched my bodily thirst, but I knew my soul had a different one that needed quenching. The sky clouded over again, with more strong gusts of south wind. I could be in for some wet riding the next day.

I awakened easily at five-thirty the next morning and started to pack-up the tent and the rest of my gear. The weather was relatively calm, and I thought the day would be a great one for cycling. I walked my bike to the top of the hill towards the camp office, washroom, and exit. Within minutes the weather worsened. I stood in the doorway of the washroom and looked at my bike, loaded down with gear, leaning against the small building.

The sky darkened, and thick, oppressive clouds descended. Within a few seconds of my noticing the change, the wind picked up. In a meteorological catharsis, huge raindrops splashed on the ground. As the storm started, it showed no signs of quickly blowing through. I stood and watched the weather from that bathroom doorway for quite a long time. When I put my hand out to feel the rain, thick drops of hard, warm water pelted my skin. Again, the ferocious wind bent tree limbs in unnatural directions. Cycling on this day would be impossible, if not miserable.

A man had been watching the dramatic weather change, and my state of inertia. Shaving kit under one arm, towel draped around his neck, the seventy-year old made his way toward me.

"Hello, there. Here's a cup of coffee and a couple danishes. I don't think you're going anywhere today."

"Wow, man, thanks!"

"Don't mention it. My name's Everil Pitkin."

"Good to meet you Everil, I'm Pat. Yep, the weather looks pretty bad. I think you're right. I'll be here for another day."

Pitkin set his burning cigarette on the edge of the sink. Watching him shaving, carefully stretching his wrinkled skin and deftly missing raised moles, I answered his many questions about the journey I was on. Our conversation touched upon Canada, the U.S., Ontario's socialized health plan, and the state of youth growing up in our ever-changing society.

His cigarette smoke curled past his squinting eye. He caught me studying him. "Ah, yeah, I know I shouldn't be smokin' these darn things, but I already got a heart and lung condition, so I figure too late to quit now. I don't suppose you ever smoked?"

"Nope. Never smoked a cigarette."

"Didn't think so. Ya look too healthy pedaling that bike an' all. Pat, the weather's looking bad. Might change. Might not. Why don't you join me in my RV for more coffee."

In the RV, Pitkin lit up another cigarette.

"Is the smoke gonna bother you?"

"Nope," I said. Mom had smoked when we were younger. We had hounded her until she quit. The smell of cigarette smoke was still irritating, but I was a guest in Pitkin's home.

I noticed the deep yellow-orange nicotine stains on his right thumb and index finger. Pitkin's demeanor remained happy as he drew hard on his cigarette and then proceeded to describe the government housing where he used to live.

"Do you know many *blacks*, Patrick?"

"No, not too many." I had known a couple of blacks at the all-boys Jesuit High School I had attended in Ohio. Memories of witnessing Max and Guy interact as minority students in the school were still fresh. I had known Max well enough to say "hello" as we passed in the hallway, but by virtue of their skin color, he and Guy were different. They were treated differently too. Some boys would spew vitriolic disdain for their presence. The majority of the school's attendees demonstrated a nervous attempt to gain their attention and acceptance. *Why is Pitkin suddenly making reference to blacks?*

Pitkin said, "You know, they smell different."

He picked up on my incredulous facial expression. *This guy is a bloody racist. I need to get out of here.* Instead, I sat and listened, trapped in my own insecurities telling me to remain polite and not cause a scene.

"That's why they wear so much perfume and deodorant," he said. The coffee began to churn in my stomach. I wasn't used to someone talking to me about another group of people in such a degrading tone.

"I know all about *blacks*, because I was the only *whitey* in the projects. Have you ever had intercourse with a woman, Patrick?"

My eyebrows rose. I was now completely stunned. He dragged hard on his cigarette. I wanted to bolt out of his RV like a rabbit running from a fox. I needed to distance myself from this dreadful man.

"Sex is no different," he said, "no better, no worse than with a white girl. I know, because I had me some *black* pussy in the projects. Pussy is pussy, and while you are young you can never get enough."

My eyes widened under my still raised brows. Pitkin quickly changed the subject.

"Patrick, do you go to church?"

"Yeah." Pause. "I'm Roman Catholic." Since I had not attended church in over a year, my answer felt like a lie. *How am I gonna get out of here? Do I push him over, bolt out the RV door, and run for my bike? No. This won't last long. Just sit quietly and wait for the right opportunity to say thanks and goodbye.*

"I went to the Church of the Nazarene," he said; "but no church is better than any other, and there's nothing wrong with you attending the Roman Catholic Church."

"It seems to me," I said, "that we're all praying to the same God, regardless of the religion." I shifted, uneasy now, in his RV kitchen chair.

"My son married an RC and then he became an RC himself."

The reference to marriage had my stomach reeling with the fear that the conversation would once again denigrate to sex or racism or some other mean-spirited topic.

Pitkin obviously knew I was no longer willing to join him in any diatribe. "Pat, I'm heading to the next town down the road, Arcade. Do you want to put your bike in here for the ride?"

"No, thanks, Mr. Pitkin." I rose from my chair. "Thanks for the coffee and danishes."

"Wait just a minute, Patrick. I have a gift for you." Pitkin showed his age more than ever as he stood and shuffled his way over to a drawer in the RV. He pulled out a small book about Jesus' parables, put out by the Church of the Nazarene. I was familiar with similar Catholic booklets. He handed me the booklet and said that it was nice to meet me.

"Thanks." I walked out of his RV back to my freedom.

I spent the next couple of hours in the camp store, listening for weather reports on a crackling radio, and browsing through magazines. My thoughts continually drifted back to Pitkin and my Roman Catholic upbringing.

The old boy Catholic priests would have loved to see me become a priest. When I was a teenager in Ohio, the local young priest would come by our home with the excuse of, "I'd like to shoot some baskets with you, Pat." Mom and Dad were obviously in on the ruse, and Mom questioned me at the dinner table.

"Pat, did you enjoy Father Mike coming to play some basketball with you?"

"Yeah. It was all right, I guess..."

"What do you mean *all right?* What did the two of you talk about?"

"He was asking if I might like to go to the seminary, and if I ever thought of becoming a priest."

"Well, son, what did you tell him?" Dad asked.

"I don't wanna be a priest."

"I think it's pretty special having him take time out of his day to spend it with you," Mom said. "Would you like Father Mike to come-by to play ball again?"

"Nope. Not if he's gonna be buggin' me about being a priest. I'd rather just shoot baskets by myself." *Even my parents betray me to the Catholic Church. Leave basketball out of it.*

I was a quiet, daydreaming loner of a kid. Given how steeped they were in the Roman Catholic faith, I now understand Mom and Dad thinking that priesthood might be an option for their eldest son.

A few short years later though, I began to feel a new uneasiness about "men of the cloth." Brother Eweneck approached me in the hallway of my grade nine Jesuit high school in Ohio.

"Pat, I heard through the grapevine here that you're leaving us."

"Yeah. We're moving to Canada."

"How do you feel about that?"

"I don't know." I furrowed my brow, revealing the fright and confusion that the move away from my friends, school, and home was causing me at the time.

"Pat, why don't you swing by my office after Mass tomorrow. We can have a visit and talk about the move to Canada."

"Okay, but I don't know where your office is."

"Oh, right. We've never met in my office before. Just look for me in the sacristy after Mass tomorrow. Head-along to your next class now."

"See you tomorrow, Brother Eweneck." I felt special being singled out and invited to his office.

After Mass I stood awkwardly in the hallway outside of the sacristy. The priest who had said Mass came out and looked at me quizzically. "Shouldn't you be off to class?"

"No, Father, I was supposed to meet Brother Eweneck here."

"What for?"

"We were gonna have a meeting in his office."

"Okay. Just wait here. I'll see if I can locate him for you."

Minutes later, Brother Eweneck came for me. "Hi, Pat. Sorry to keep you waiting. Follow me. We'll have a visit and a cup of tea."

I followed through a maze of unfamiliar hallways.

"Here we are, Pat. Come on in." Brother Eweneck unlocked the door to his office. "Excuse the clutter in here."

The windowless office was dark. Eweneck quickly turned on a dim desk lamp.

"Where should I sit?"

"Yeah, that looks to be a problem." Chuckling to himself, he moved a pile of books from a chair beside his desk. I sat down. "Now, Pat, what do you take in your tea?"

"A little milk and sugar, please. Thanks."

"Coming right up. The kitchen is just down the hall. Make yourself comfortable."

I studied the inside of the room. Dark, dank, lifeless. A photo of the pontiff hung on one wall along with a crucifix. On another wall was a Monet print of pastel flowers that seemed to be swallowed up by the room's aura. Various theology, history, and psychology books filled the bookshelves lining the rest of the room. Another stack of books sat on the desk along with files containing papers of unknown content.

As I traced the various titles stacked next to me with my finger, the door opened to Eweneck. Setting down a tray with two cups of tea, two spoons, a sugar bowl, and a plate of cookies, Brother Eweneck asked, "Do you like books, Pat?"

"Kinda."

"What have you read lately?"

"Mostly school books, but the last book outside of school was *Serpico*."

"That title rings a bell with me. Tell me about it."

"It's about a New York City cop who uncovers corruption within the police department."

"Oh, yeah. Hey, that's pretty heavy stuff for a young guy like you."

I shrugged, took a sip of the hot tea and then reached for a cookie.

"So, Pat, tell me about this move to Canada."

"My Dad's job is taking us there. We leave this summer. I think the town is St. Thomas, Ontario."

"St. Thomas? Have you looked for it on a map?"

"No."

Brother Eweneck rose and studied the bookshelves until he found an atlas. The binding crackled like dry leaves, breaking the silence in the room. "Let's take a look. Pull your chair around next to me, Pat."

Obeying, I sat next to him as he slowly, gently turned the pages. His action had a hypnotic effect. "*Hmmm,*" he said. As he leaned toward me he slowly caressed a page. "Ontario. Here. I think you'll find it here somewhere. Take a look." His voice became a whisper.

Leaning over the page, I searched for the town of St. Thomas. Brother Eweneck gently touched my back with his hand. His warm breath was now on my neck.

This doesn't feel right.

Another whisper, "It's okay, Pat, you have nothing to fear."

What's he talking about? The move? Him?

There was uneasiness in the pit of my stomach that conflicted with the freshly consumed tea and cookies. The tension of the room was suddenly broken by the sound of a key unlocking the door. Brother Eweneck pulled his hand away from my back. In walked another Jesuit Brother.

"Sorry to interrupt, I thought the room was unoccupied. I see you have a new friend, Brother Eweneck."

New friend? This doesn't feel or sound right. This is creepy.

"Yes. This is young Patrick Milroy. He will be soon leaving us for Canada."

"Canada. Wow, that's a move!"

"Look at the time. Pat, you better run along to your next class."

"Yeah. Okay. Thanks for the tea." I rose and headed for the door.

"Pat, come back and visit me again. We'll talk more about your move to Canada. I want you to consider me a good friend. Can you make your way back to the school? Down this hallway, right, left, right through the doors, and you're in the hallway near the chapel."

My head swam with alarm as I walked back to school. *Stay away from him. Don't go for another visit.* I obeyed my inner voice.

Roman Catholicism was deeply ensconced within the families of both my parents. Mom hailed from Duluth, Minnesota, and Dad from the bordering town of Superior, Wisconsin. Craggy rocks, dense forest, and unpredictable waters were the setting for the Jesuit missionaries who were ushered into Northeastern Minnesota and Northwestern Wisconsin by French voyageurs in the seventeenth century.

In 1875 the Vicariate of Northern Minnesota was established to meet the spiritual needs of immigrants and American Indians. Pope Leo XIII declared the northern half of the vicariate as the Diocese of Duluth in 1875. The Diocese of Superior was established by Pope Pius X in 1905. The harshness of the land was mirrored by a rugged Roman Catholic doctrine.

All of Christianity can trace itself back to the lifetime of Jesus Christ. After the crucifixion, death, and resurrection of Jesus, the disciples heralded the Apostolic or New Testament Age from the year thirty to the year one-hundred-twenty. Christians believe in one God who manifests himself in three persons, or the Trinity: the Father, Son, and Holy Spirit.

The word *catholic* means "all inclusive" or "universal." Roman Catholics trace their historical founding to Jesus' words:

> [18] And I also say to you that you are Peter, and on this rock I will build My church, and the gates of Hades shall not prevail against it. [19] And I will give you the keys of the kingdom of heaven, and whatever you bind on earth will be bound in heaven, and whatever you loose on earth will be loosed in heaven."
> *Matthew 16:18-19 NKJV*

Aramaic was the language Jesus and his twelve Apostles spoke. The word *Peter* and the word *rock* were the same in Aramaic. Roman Catholic tradition declared that Peter was the first Pope or *Father*.

In my childhood I heard, "on the rock of Peter, Jesus founded the Church" and "Children, you're learning the truth; there is no need to question." They didn't teach me that the successors of Peter did not use the theological hierarchy of Pope until the third century.

Protestant Christians have interpreted Matthew 16:18-19 to mean that the church is founded upon Jesus as the Messiah, the Son of God.

Was Peter really the first Pope? Jesus often taught using parables. Maybe the rock that Jesus was referring to was a metaphor for the earth. Yeah, that seems to make a lot more sense to me. Interpreting Peter as the first Pope seems just plain ludicrous in the face of the Roman Catholic tradition, disposed to power, greed, and avarice. Papal infallibility is built upon the very premise of "to bind and to loose." Permit, approve, or forbid. As the first Pope, Peter had this earthly authority.

Was Peter the only one given the power to bind and loose on earth? Seems too contrived. Peter declared Jesus the Son of God. That was a huge declaration of faith. Maybe Jesus meant the individual believer, through faith, had the power to bind and loose.

[18] "Assuredly, I say to you, whatever you bind on earth will be bound in heaven, and whatever you loose on earth will be loosed in heaven. [19] "Again I say to you that if two of you agree on earth concerning anything that they ask, it will be done for them by My Father in heaven. [20] For where two or three are gathered together in My name, I am there in the midst of them."
Matthew 18:18-20 NKJV

"Where two or three are gathered" the Catholic founders kinda skipped over that one by declaring the Pope to be Christ's authority on earth. No matter, 'cause I don't have that kinda faith. Still, this trip is a spiritual journey.

Is God trying to reach me through a person like Pitkin? Maybe, because Pitkin handed me a book on Jesus' parables, I should be learning more about Jesus. Lots of people have talked about God speaking and working through others. But why would God allow a message to be mixed with racism and sexism?

I do believe in God, who loves me unconditionally, who created me and created the universe, but do I need to believe in Jesus? Why can't I just go on believing in God? Why can't I continue to experience God through nature and in other loving individuals?

Sister Mary, my English teacher at my Catholic High School in St. Thomas, had called what I was going through an identity crisis. She was right. I really did not know what I was to do in this life. *I do sense that I am here for a purpose, but what purpose?*

I had a special connection to Sister Mary. Happy eyes that danced from a narrow face contrasted with her quiet and gentle way. In her English class I strove to do my best.

Sister Mary was transferred from her teaching post in St. Thomas to a hospice care posting in London, Ontario. The residence that she lived in with other nuns was close to the campus of the University of Western Ontario where I was studying Physical Education. We had met a few times for lunch or coffee. When my crisis about life, spirituality, and relationships all collided, Sister Mary had listened.

"You know, Sister Mary, as a kid, I was never allowed to question the Catholic Church. This adult free-choice stuff versus my childhood indoctrination is a big revelation for me."

"Some people never question their faith," she said. "Others do, and they either become stronger or drift away. Pat, you may never go back to the Roman Catholic Church. You're on a spiritual journey, and you need to see where that journey takes you."

"No one ever said that to me before. So it's okay for me to be questioning all of this stuff?" A lump had formed in my throat.

"Okay? Pat, it's more than *okay*. Our spiritual being is the most important part of our lives. You have to keep searching."

The woman at the register of the camp store and I focused our attention on the radio announcer's forecast, which called for clearing by midnight. She rented the campsite back to me for four dollars instead of the usual fee of eight.

After buying some food, I set up the tent between cloudbursts. The ground was soaked and the grass spongy. Water quickly soaked through the bottom of the tent. The rest of my gear was dripping with water from being on the bike in the rain.

By nightfall, I lay in a cold and damp tent. Low clouds and intermittent downpours accompanied strong gusts of wind. The fiberglass poles of the small tent bent with the wind, sometimes pushing the mosquito netting and tent fly down on me. The tent was designed to keep the fly from touching the inner netting, but it was no match for the gusting winds. Water dripped on me. I lay there thinking; *no better time to contemplate life.*

Did God make the weather bad today just for my sake? It feels too coincidental to not be from a higher power; but why would God make the weather so terrible just for my sake, when a storm causes difficulty and even suffering for other people? Are incidents in life attributed to divine intervention, fate, or mere coincidence? Which is it?

If God loves me unconditionally, then it makes perfect sense that God would intervene to guide me in life. God, however, supposedly gave me my life to do with it what I choose. Can I accept that God wants to guide me to make the best choices and to find my mission in life?

What does Jesus have to do with all of this? Why do people worship Jesus? Does Jesus have anything to do with my

mission in life? Jesus taught humanity how to love uncondi-
tionally. I believe that all humanity is called to love.

I recalled Richard Bach's *Jonathan Livingston Seagull*.
Jonathan, as a seagull, discovered that the main reason he was
given life as a bird was to fly — and to fly to his ultimate potential. *Yeah, love, that's it! Love is our ultimate potential. But*
what does it entail? What am I called to do, as I attempt to
fulfill my mission to love?

My thoughts once again turned to a memory of Sister Mary
putting my mind at ease by saying, "Patrick, I think you are
being drawn to some calling." Her words rang true to me.

Am I being called to be a medical doctor, a doctor of chiro-
practic, or have I already found that calling in the work I had
been doing with the group home for the disabled? How do I
obtain a confirmation of my mission in life?

I pulled the sleeping bag up around my shoulders and repo-
sitioned my body in the wet tent. The light, steady rain hitting
the tent fly had a sedative effect. Within seconds I drifted into
sleep.

After a bone-chilling, wet sleep, the rising sun gradually
warmed me. My rested legs welcomed the change of workload,
even pedaling during the downhill ride into Angelica. *This is*
a pretty little place. That's probably how its name originated.

Highway 19.

Just keep pedaling through Angelica, don't stop.

My skin prickled and my limbs vibrated as I rode along the
dirt road toward Jones Pond. My feet, knees, arms, and hands
all ached after the bumpy ride along the eleven miles.

Ruth, with grey-streaked black hair and olive skin, the co-
owner of the campsite, extended a hand of introduction.

"Where are you coming from?"

"I got stuck in Java Canter for two nights 'cause of the storm.
I'm from Canada, and on my way to Florida."

"What will you do in Florida?"

"My Grandparents live in Largo, Florida, near St. Petersburg and Clearwater. I'll be staying with them for a bit."

Ruth's eyes brimmed with shallow tears. "I have a grandson, but we don't get along very well. He's seventeen, but he won't talk to me because I'm too old."

I clumsily tried to console her, telling her that the strain in their relationship was only temporary. "Ruth, my stuff is soaked. Do you have a dryer here?"

"You just pull out your wet gear and hand it over to me. I'll take care of it for ya."

"Thanks. That'll be great."

Ruth watched as I pulled my wet clothing from the panniers and my sleeping bag from its sack. "My, you're a sweet one, Patrick. I want you to consider me your adopted grandmother. Would that be okay with you?"

Nodding, I smiled back.

Ruth then disappeared into the laundry room while I put up my wet tent. A cool dry breeze quickly dried it.

Ruth returned with a basket of my clothes neatly folded. Holding up my newly fluffed, dry summer sleeping bag she said, "Pat, it gets real cold up here at night. This won't keep you warm enough."

"Oh, I don't know. I think I'll be okay."

"Here, sweetie, take this sheet. I'm a camper from way back. A simple cotton sheet can really keep you warm. And, no, I don't want it back! These mountains can get darn cold at night."

The clear starlit sky of the night ushered a plunge in temperature. On Sunday morning, September fourteen, I woke to find the outside of my tent frozen in a thin sheet of ice. I was ever so grateful to Ruth, her kindness, and the simple cotton sheet cocooning me in the warmth of my own body.

Gearing up, the goodbye with her was bittersweet. As she watched me pedal off, I sensed that the pain in her heart would return, after the brief respite of her grandmothering me.

III
The Broken Axle

³ Then I went down to the potter's house, and, there he was, making something at the wheel. ⁴And the vessel that he made of clay was marred in the hand of the potter; so he made it again into another vessel, as seemed good to the potter to make it. ⁵ Then the word of the LORD came to me, saying: ⁶ "O house of Israel, can I not do with you as this potter?" says the LORD. "Look, as the clay is in the potter's hand, so are you in My hand, O house of Israel."
Jeremiah 18:3-6 NKJV

The ride from Jones Pond to Highway 19 was bumpy and mostly downhill. The road was engulfed in a thick fog barely permitting a twenty-foot visibility. As the fog burned off, I saw signs for churches of all denominations peppering the roadside. *This is it! I'll worship God's creation through the experience and appreciation of riding. I don't need a church today.* The turn of the pedals, my steady breathing, and the changing scenery – this was all a meditation unto itself.

Highway 19 became Pennsylvania State Road 449. I pedaled through the towns of Genesee, Hickox, and Gold. Each town was a goal, and all the while the road became steeper, with Galeton, Pennsylvania along Highway 6 the final goal for the day. Each hill was a challenge of long climbs rewarded by sweet coasts down the other sides.

At the Ox Yoke Inn Campground, I pitched my tent on ground thick with needles from the surrounding conifers. The campsite was beside a creek that danced melodiously over rocks. After enjoying the warmth of a campfire, I fell into a deep sleep, as I felt the nutrition of a steak dinner fuel and strengthen my aching, tired legs.

The next morning, just out of Galetown, I was climbing a very steep, winding road up the side of a mountain. *Keep going Pat. You can do it.* I rocked the bike side to side during the climb. *Make it to the top without stopping.* My chest heaved with big gulps of air. *Don't stop. Ignore the burn in your legs. Keep going.* Every switchback showed me a new vista of lush forest, with green moss, ferns, and low shrubs lining the road. Trees with branches extending toward the road greeted me with each rotation of the wheel. *Another switchback. Keep going.* Around the next turn, blue sky broke the green walls around me. I knew the summit was close. *The top. I made it! Didn't stop once. Way to go!* I coasted down the other side into a town.

Outside of Germania I started another steeper, tougher climb. *Keep pumping, Pat. Just one pedal turn at a time.* I pulled hard on the handlebars to leverage more effort onto the pedals. My legs were aching. *Come on, man, don't stop. Dig deep. Keep going.*

Frothy drool now dropped from my gaping mouth as I sucked in air. *Almost there. Don't stop. You can do it.* At the crest of the mountain pass I coasted toward the large sign listing the elevation as 2,175 feet. A sense of personal accomplishment sent a chill down my spine. I took a picture of my bike with the sign, and another of the view, peeking out over a carpet of thickly treed valley and other mountains crowding the horizon.

Highway 44 undulated on top of that mountain range for many more miles. Tall trees formed a green canopy over the road. No traffic. I was reveling in my effort, freedom, and sense of self.

What's that up ahead? A deer leisurely walked onto the road thirty feet in front of me. I slowed to a quick, quiet stop. When I stopped, the doe stopped. *Stay there, sweetie.* I reached for my camera in my handlebar pack. *Don't go.* She calmly entered the woods. I inched my bike up to where she had entered. *There you are. Don't move. Let me take your picture.* She posed about ten yards in front of me. I clicked the camera shutter. Her long ears were perked toward me. Silence, and then she turned and walked deeper into her forest home. Time stood still. *Thank you.* The peaceful scenery, wildlife, and physical effort of my body seemed to be the essence of God's presence.

Seven miles of coasting down the mountainside was my reward for the hard climb. I gripped the handlebars hard against the bike's vibration as my speed steadily rose. I leaned the bike into descending switchbacks. *Something doesn't feel right. Where is this sluggishness coming from?* I checked the front brakes. They were fine. The rear brakes were working well too. Pushing the pedals hard, I watched the rear wheel track off center near the bottom bracket. *Broken spoke? Bent rim? Just get to the campground ahead in Waterville.*

Gear unloaded, tent up, tools out. The quick release mechanism was warm to my touch as I removed my rear wheel. *That's strange.* Taking the quick release out of the axle, I tipped the wheel on its side. With a slight tap, the hot metal of the rear axle fell into my hand in two pieces.

Happy Acres Campground was owned by Charlie. At his camp store I showed him the broken axle. "This is the rear axle from my bike. I don't know what I'm gonna do."

"Pat, just wait here a few minutes. We'll look through my box of spare bike parts."

The box contained worn brake pads, brake levers, an old derailleur, several pedals, and various nuts and bolts. Charlie paused and again looked at the broken axle.

"Nothing that looks like that in here."

"Do ya know of any bike shops close by?"

"I think the closest is Duffy's in Avis."

"How far is Avis?"

"Oh, 'bout ten miles down the road. Here's the phone book. Give them a call, and see if they can help you out."

A young lady answered the telephone at Duffy's. "I'm sure we can help you. I'll give you our home phone number. If you completely break down, I'll come an' get you with my truck."

Charlie saw my face relax as I spoke to the Duffy's lady.

"Looks like you got some good news, Pat."

"Yep. They can help me."

"Do you want a ride there?"

"I think I can manage to get there on the bike. Heck, its only ten miles, so I can walk there if I can't ride."

"These mountains can be hard on people and their machines, Pat. We get a lot of groups and couples bicycling through these parts, but not too many traveling alone like you. Where you going from here?"

"I'd like to see Gettysburg."

Charlie pulled out a Pennsylvania camping directory and map. "Good cycling this way." With a strong finger he traced on the map a route through the mountains.

The ride into Avis was slow. The broken axle was secured only by the tightening of the quick release. Pedaling hard caused the rear wheel to continue tracking wrong. The ten miles took me over two hours. I was in Avis by mid-morning, but Duffy's bike shop would not be open until one in the afternoon.

At Carm's Restaurant, I studied my maps over tea.

"What can I get you from the kitchen?"

"I'll start with two of your breakfast specials." The dollar-ninety-nine breakfast was an easy way to fuel up for the day.

"Are you *that* hungry?" The tired looking waitress took an interest in my big appetite and mode of travel.

"Oh yeah. Riding through these mountains, I work up a good appetite."

The four eggs, four pieces of toast, and six slices of bacon went down fast.

"You were hungry. More tea, honey?"

"Yeah, more tea would be great. Actually, I'm still hungry. Could I get one more breakfast special?"

"I'd be as big as a house if I ate like you; but I guess you'll be burning it all off. Okay! Comin' right up!"

Duffy's bike shop was a busy place. All of the young kids from the town seemed to be hanging out. Brenda, the owner's daughter whom I had spoken to on the telephone, welcomed me. I watched her run her parents' shop – loaning tools to the young kids, talking shop, and working the cash register. When the store quieted down, Brenda assisted me in the repair of my bike.

The friction of the broken axle had worn a small hole through the wheel's rear hub. We emptied a box of spare used parts and identified an axle that would work. I studied the used part. "Brenda, do you think I should replace the entire wheel?"

She tilted her head at my query, and her auburn, shoulder-length hair fell over her shoulder, pronouncing her country-girl charm. "You could, but that'd be expensive, and even though there's a small hole in the hub, this axle should keep you going. Actually, if my husband Rob were here, he'd be able to tell you if your wheel would work with the hole in the hub. It might be alright all the way to Florida, or it might give you trouble a mile down the road. I'm just not sure."

I looked up at the ceiling and studied the bright, shiny new wheels hanging there.

No, that used axle won't do. Don't take a chance. Spend money on a new wheel. "What's the best wheel up there?"

Brenda studied the wheels with me. "Let's try that one."

My tube and tire were put on the new wheel, only for us to discover the new wheel wasn't true.

"My brother can true the wheel. He gets off work later and should be here by six-thirty."

The time passed slowly as I walked around the quiet town of Avis. Brenda and her husband Rob invited me to join their dinner of cooked chicken and macaroni salad from the local Minimart. The greasy chicken quickly filled me up. Shortly after dinner Brenda's brother Darren arrived at the shop.

I looked over Darren's shoulder as he methodically spun the new wheel, tightening some spokes and loosening others. Sitting up he put both hands on his thighs and shrugged.

"Sorry, man. Can't be trued. This wheel has a warp in it. It's garbage. Let's try another."

The only other wheel in the shop had a solid axle without a quick release mechanism, and was clearly inferior to my damaged one.

"You could just use your own wheel until the next town. It's still a good wheel. I wouldn't worry much about the little hole in the hub."

"That's what I thought," Brenda said, smiling.

"It's up to you, though. You could save yourself some money."

I had discarded the notion of using my damaged but still usable wheel earlier in the day.

"No. I'm going with the new one."

"Okay. I'll have it on in no time, and I'll give you a good deal on it."

Darren installed the new wheel and then proceeded to tune-up my brakes and gears, lube my chain, and check my tire pressure. Long shadows had become darkness in Avis, so Rob gave me a ride to the Susquehanna Campground in Jersey Shore.

I left Jersey Shore, Pennsylvania mid-morning the next day. Though the sun was shining, it was very chilly out, and stayed cool most of the day. I cycled from Jersey Shore to Locke Haven where I stopped and ate a big breakfast.

The terrain was not too bad in the morning except for the steep ride up Mount Nittany. At the top I took a picture of my bike with the elevation marker – another proof of achievement.

Those Allegany Mountain roads, like the roads further north, were characterized by extreme grades with rewarding vistas at the summits, overlooking leafy woodlands. *Suffer with the effort on the way up the mountains; bask in pure joy coasting down. Too bad the suffering lasts longer than the ride down. It seems kinda like life. Try to enjoy the scenery regardless of the pain or the pleasure.*

I chose a route through the Allegany's that would bring me through a Pennsylvania town sharing my uncommon surname, Milroy; and on the highway just outside of Milroy, I coasted my bike to a stop. The "Welcome to Milroy" sign was made up of six smaller signs, each displaying the name of a church: United Methodist Church, St. Paul Evangelical Lutheran Church, White Memorial United Church of Christ, Milroy Grace Brethren Church, United Presbyterian Church, and the Christian Missionary Alliance.

Hmmm, there's no Catholic church. Maybe that's no coincidence. Maybe God's not caught up in the denomination issue.

The old wooden floor of the Milroy Library creaked as I entered. The silence of the room was broken by a tentative, "Can I help you?" as I approached the checkout counter. I could tell my cycling attire and sweat-drenched T-shirt caught the lone librarian off-guard.

"Hi. I'm curious about the founding of this town. You see, my last name is Milroy."

Brushing her grey hair behind her ears, the elderly librarian slowly rose from her desk and approached the counter. Her

long blue dress was tented above black shoes and heavy, an-
kle-bunched nylon stockings.

"We don't get many people coming in here and asking about
that."

Another librarian emerged from the stacks. She wore the
same attire.

"This young man is asking about the founding of the town."

"My word! We haven't had anyone ask about our town's
name in years. I know we have some news clippings and a
write-up about it somewhere in here."

"We had another Milroy stop buy here years ago."

"Do you remember his name?" I asked.

"I remember he was from Superior, Wisconsin," she said
pausing and then added, "I think his name was Phillip."

"Phillip! He's my uncle! My name's Pat. My family lives in
Canada now." I gently shook their hands.

"My, oh my, what a small world! Now, let me answer your
question about the town. It's named after Henry Milroy who
once owned the land this town is built on. Henry was a militia
soldier in the Revolution. They say those Milroy's are related to
Robert the Bruce of Scotland. One of Robert the Bruce's grand-
sons was named John McElroy. John fled Scotland, changed
his name to Milroy and settled near Carlisle, Pennsylvania.
Henry was John Milroy's son."

"Wow. That's pretty neat history! I've heard of Robert the
Bruce, but I don't know much about him."

"He followed in the footsteps of William Wallace in seeking independence from England. Robert was successful and
became the first King of Scotland. He had quite a reputation as
a statesman, and as a military leader who used brutality." She
paused. "It's a pretty rich history. Pat, do you think your family
is related to the Henry Milroy lineage?"

"Don't think so, but if we are it would be way back in
Scotland."

The two volunteer librarians broke their rule to stay at their desks until closing time, and obliged me by walking outside to take a picture of me with my bike in front of the library.

I went to a pay phone, called home, and then rode to the Milroy Variety Store and bought a carton of chocolate milk. The store was right across from the Milroy Hose Company – the local fire hall. The librarians and store clerk were the only three people whom I saw in the little town, which made it seem abandoned, yet with a secret allure.

Leaving Milroy, I continued along Highway 322. Heavy traffic made the ride treacherous. The shoulder of the highway offered only a slight refuge from the cars and trucks whizzing past me. To my joy, however, the scenery along Highway 322 opened into large expanses of sky above sloping and rolling woodland. I stopped and took several pictures.

Fatigue, mixed with a sense of accomplishment and contentment filled me as I set up the tent. Dinner at a local pizza shop replenished my body's drained energy. It did not seem to matter what I ate. My body put it all to good use. *Try to make it as far as Gettysburg tomorrow.* I drifted into sleep hoping I would wake up early in the morning.

IV
God Bless America

¹¹ By the blessing of the upright the city is exalted, but it is overthrown by the mouth of the wicked.
¹² He that is devoid of wisdom despises his neighbor, but a man of understanding holds his peace.
¹³A talebearer reveals secrets, but he that is of a faithful spirit conceals a matter.
¹⁴ Where there is no counsel, the people fall; but in the multitude of counselors there is safety.
Proverbs 11:11-14 NKJV

Heavy dew covered the grass and tent when I awoke at five-thirty. After a quick trip to the men's room, I elected to crawl back into my sleeping bag and wrap myself up in sheets. Once I was cocooned in my body's warmth, I dozed off for a couple more hours. I had wanted to leave Walker's Campground much earlier, hoping the sun would quickly dry the dew-soaked tent, yet it had not burned its way through the foggy-looking clouds. Eventually I packed up the wet tent and headed out.

My first stop was at the Mexico, Pennsylvania post office to mail the letter I wrote to my sister Amy last night; and then I stopped in Post Royal to fuel my body with breakfast at a small diner. The riding was tough again. My legs were still tired from yesterday's ride. I pedaled on, even though it was slow going.

The day's ride took me up and down two mountains. My bike was always in first gear as the road snaked its way to the top. Both mountains had signs reading *"Eight percent grade for two-and-one-half miles."* The sweat poured from my body on the way up the mountains. At one point I swiped my brow on my shirtsleeve only to notice a thick salty froth. As I climbed upward the pouring sweat dripped across my lips. I parted them with my tongue to taste salty, bitter sweat making me think I was cleansing my body of deep toxins. The seeping sweat stung my eyes as if I was cutting yellow onions with a dull knife. The ride was long, slow and hard, but, oh, so reward-ing when I finally made it to the top. The ride down the other side, also sporting an eight-percent grade, was so fast that the frame of my bike vibrated.

On the south side of each mountain I crossed were verdant valleys. I took pictures, but the hazy sky did not do justice to what my eyes and other senses took privilege in admiring. *Surely God created all this. People who do not believe in God must have some sort of inner pain.*

Gettysburg was my initial goal for the day's ride. I might have made it had I left two hours earlier as planned, but instead I stopped at the Moyer Mountain Retreat, a campground nes-tled on the south side of a small mountain just outside of Mount Holly Springs. Rain began just as I pulled into the campground, so Mr. Moyer, the campground owner, let me sleep on the out-door stage. I had explained to him that my tent was already soaked from the previous night. Since the stage faced away from the prevailing wind and rain, three walls and a roof over my head were almost complete protection. The shelter of the stage also allowed me to rig a makeshift clothesline for hanging and drying my tent.

A hot shower warmed my muscle-fatigued body. The rain had been falling steadily since my arrival and shortly after seven o'clock; the clouds and surrounding mountains vanquished the sun's light. I looked out at the heavy raindrops creating concentric rings rippling outward in the gathering puddles on the lawn of the campground. The rings blended with one another, being engulfed and re-formed by the drops. *Does God have a message for me in those drops and rings of puddled water? The rings rippling from each drop affect all the rings of those around it. Is this what we do to each other?*

I rolled my sleeping bag out on the stage, which was covered with a well-worn green outdoor carpet. The cool air, wind, and rain kept mosquitoes away. As I lay in the sleeping bag, I thought about all the people I had met thus far. Good and friendly folk. It was such a boost to hear "Good luck," and "Have a safe trip." *People tend to treat me differently, not just because of the bike, but because I'm traveling alone. I hope the weather clears overnight.* I drifted off in my thoughts. I was warm, dry, and very content with the campground stage, but deep sleep would not come to me.

When it finally did, it lasted until eight in the morning. I woke to see a dense fog covering Moyer's Mountain Retreat. Taking my time, I wrote a few postcards and a letter, occasionally looking skyward for the sun to burn off the fog.

Following directions from a man who lived off Highway 97, I weaved my way back to Highway 34. My legs were still very tired, and my right knee was sore. Thankfully, Gettysburg was only about a twenty-mile ride from Moyer's. I made a stop at the small town of Bendersville to mail the letters and postcards that I'd written, and, after a lunch, I headed straight for the Gettysburg National Park Visitor's Center.

There I met another bicycle tourist, Larry, who was on his way home to Washington, D.C. from a bike trip in Nova Scotia and P.E.I. Larry gave me his address and invited me to stay on my way through. The invite was genuine, but I was committed to the idea of a bed and breakfast in DC. After inquiring about the local Gettysburg campgrounds, I went to the Artillery Ridge Campground, only one mile from the Visitor's Center.

I set up my tent on flat grassy ground, dwarfed by the RV at the adjacent site. A retired couple emerged from the RV and, after introductions, they brought me a couple of jelly donuts and asked me all sorts of questions about my journey.

On the camp pay phone, I contacted and made arrangements for John Ross's B&B in Washington, D.C. I hoped the next day's weather would be nice enough for a good tour of Gettysburg.

My battlefield tour started fairly early. The fields where so many had fallen were covered in a light, cool fog. At times I felt someone was standing behind me watching me, only to turn and find myself alone. There seemed to be a kind of electricity in the air reaching out to me. From June thirtieth to July third of 1863, the Confederate and Union Armies had battled at Gettysburg. Since more than fifty-one thousand men had lost their lives here, it was easy for me to imagine the souls of some of them walking the fields of Gettysburg.

The magnitude of lost lives, dreams never fulfilled, and countrymen killing one another was difficult to comprehend in the face of my life's blessings. I toured the battlefield feeling overwhelmed by the sacrifices of the fallen and the attempt to memorialize the battle. As I absorbed the solemnity of the place, part of me longed to be with someone – yet I knew I needed this time to myself.

When I returned to the campground, I busied myself by writing more postcards. I also struck up a conversation with the couple. Charlie and Gerry expressed their admiration of my trip. It turned out we had something in common. Charlie had been born in Minneapolis, Minnesota. Now retired, they lived in San Diego, California, and traveled around the U.S. in their RV.

Shortly after our visit Gerry brought over a baked potato smothered in butter with just a sprinkle of pepper. The hot, starchy, moist potato seemed to nourish me in a way I most definitely needed. As I was about to finish eating, she came over with a bowl of fresh, homemade coleslaw that was equally wholesome.

I sat and thought about all the RVs and their retired owners in the camp. It would be a really nice way to retire: to have an RV, and be financially secure. I daydreamed of spending three months at four different campsites in a year. *I would use whatever campsite I was at as a home base, so I'd be able to cycle out to different places. I would see so much of the country this way and I'd see it up close. I would meet lots of people, see many hidden wonderful places, get plenty of exercise, and I'd feel very close to God's creation. Wow, that would be great.* My daydream ended with the thought that I wouldn't want to do it alone.

On September twenty-one I cycled through thick fog that caused water to collect on my glasses. It lent a ghostly sense of mystery to Gettysburg.

Late in the morning, I stopped at a convenience store in Sunshine, Pennsylvania. As I stood outside of the convenience store, replenishing fluids and having a snack, a couple on a tandem bike rolled up. Within minutes four or five more cyclists arrived. They asked about my trip and offered words of encouragement. I felt good meeting them. They were all members of the Baltimore Bicycle Club.

I called John Ross's B&B from Sunshine, Pennsylvania. John had left a taped message for me saying that he would be home in the afternoon. I left Sunshine and was in Washington, D.C. at his address by just after noon. *Wow, I made it! – All the way through the state of Maryland in one day!*

All I could do was wait. Sitting on his front porch, I noticed the neighborhood was very ethnic. Across from the townhouses of Argonne Place where John lived was an apartment building filled with Hispanics and a few blacks. The neighborhood seemed quaint and sedate.

As I sat on John's front porch waiting, his neighbor Dave came out, introduced himself, and invited me over for a bagel and a cup of coffee. He was working on his Masters in Linguistics at Georgetown University. Dave had gone back to school at the age of thirty, and had done his undergrad in engineering science, specializing in computers. We pulled out my map of D.C. and he patiently pointed out how to get around on my bike via paths and roads.

John and I were finally introduced on Dave's front porch. Lt. Col. John Ross of the US Air Force explained that in June he would be retiring, after having served for thirty-seven years.

After a shower, I watched the Washington Redskins defeat the San Diego Chargers on TV. John was a Redskins fan. "Do you follow football, Pat? As far as I'm concerned, the Skins are America's team, not those damn Cowboys."

"Yeah, John, I follow football. Not as much as when I was younger though. I grew up in Minnesota and was a diehard Vikings fan."

"That must have been tough." I knew instantly John was referring to the run of four Super Bowl losses by the Vikings.

"Yep. Ya know I was pretty disappointed as a kid because of those four Super Bowl losses for such a great team. I idolized the 'Purple People Eaters', Allan Page, Carl Eller, their great QB Fran Tarkington and Coach Bud Grant. When we moved to Ohio when I was ten, I cheered for the Cleveland Browns. You probably remember Brian Sipes and the rest of the 'Cardiac Kids.'"

"I remember that team." John laughed as he recalled the monikers placed on the teams.

Afterward, John and I went out for an Afghanistan dinner. He assisted me in ordering the spicy food that was far removed from the meat and potatoes of my youth. The pronunciation of the various dishes rolled off his tongue with ease. I asked John if he had spent any time in Afghanistan. His face tightened and he murmured, "Oh yeah. Fascinating place, very different from

what we are used to state-side, but I can't talk much about it."
I gathered that this Lieutenant Colonel was privy to some big
secrets. We shared a bottle of wine at dinner, and then topped
it all off with ice cream at *Baskin's*.

The next morning, I woke up thinking I had not slept as
well as I thought I would, considering it was the first night I
had a bed to sleep in since leaving home. I was fully awake at
five-thirty, and just rested in bed until John called me down to
a fruit, egg, toast, and home-fries breakfast. I readied my bicycle with just the basics for touring Washington. The bike felt
somewhat awkward and ready for flight, as I pedaled without
the heavy, gear-laden panniers.

Finding a U.S. Post Office was my first goal of the day upon
leaving John's house. I stopped my bicycle on a sidewalk and
tried to orient myself with the map of DC. I felt unsure about
asking a stranger for direction. Everyone bustled past with a
got-to-get-to-work type air. Finally, a woman gave me a soft
glance as she passed.

"Excuse me, ma'am, could you tell me where I'd find the
post office?" I asked.

She looked at me with eyes that made me wonder if I'd
dripped breakfast egg yolk on my chin. I saw her pause further
as if to determine whether I was serious. In a half-sarcastic
tone she said, "You're standing right next to it." I felt my face
flush, and instantly beamed a self-amused smile at her. I was
completely oblivious to the large stone building, though I was
standing near enough to touch it. She smiled back at me and
continued walking. *Sometimes things in life are so big and so
close to me that I don't even recognize them.*

From the post office I headed to Rock Creek Park. The trees
and the trickling creek created a refuge from America's political headquarters. The paths for joggers and cyclists were well
used and in use. I didn't recall ever seeing so many people out
for a jog in one place at one time. *This must be their escape. Do
any of them talk to God the way I do?*

Eventually I made my way towards the center of Washington. I walked past the 58,022 names on the Vietnam Veterans Memorial. Some people stood touching the names of loved ones on the wall with tears streaming down their faces. Others traced a name using paper and a pencil. Flowers, flags, and other mementos decorated the foot of the Memorial. Nearby was the Frederick Hart sculpture of three American servicemen. A wave of appreciation for those who sacrificed their lives swept over me.

The Lincoln Memorial made me feel pride and give thanks for having been born an American. Lincoln's virtues of honesty, tolerance, love of justice, and charity were only realized by Americans after the assassin's bullet ended his life.

Like an artist whose genius with palate and canvas are recognized only after death, Lincoln's statesmanship was the art of his genius. What will be my legacy? Keep learning, keep searching, Pat.

I read the words inscribed in the Thomas Jefferson Memorial. "I have sworn upon the altar of God eternal hostility against every form of tyranny over the mind of man." He was a rebel. I contemplated his role in writing the Declaration of Independence. *Strange that the U.S. Constitution protects religious freedom, but so much of religion appears to be a "tyranny of the mind." And strange too, that "all Men are created equal" didn't apply to the black slaves.*

I visited the National Museum of American History and the National Air and Space Museum. *I could easily spend a week in Washington visiting memorials and museums – this is so interesting.*

Late in the afternoon I returned to John's house, retreating to my bed and journal. *It really would be nice to be sharing all of this with someone.* I closed the journal to drift off into slumber.

That evening I met John's daughter Tamara. She smiled, displaying perfect white teeth outlined by rich red lipstick. She batted her sparkling eyes as she offered to guide me around DC.

"Yeah, sure, Tamara." My voice had a noticeably nervous quiver. *Her Dad must have put in a good word about me, 'cause beautiful women don't just make offers like this to strangers.*

"Why don't we start with dinner? I know all the great restaurants," she pronounced.

Tamara and I were about the same age. She was a recent graduate of engineering from the University of Illinois. That evening, we had dinner together at an Ethiopian Restaurant with the food served in the traditional manner, without cutlery. We toasted new friends as we drank a tasty Ethiopian honey wine. After dinner we walked to *Baskin Robbins* for ice cream.

Emptiness filled me as I retreated to my room in the home of my new friend.

September twenty-three, I woke realizing I had tossed and turned my way through the night. I was again awake by five-thirty. *So much for the creature comforts of a bed. I sleep better in my tent.*

Tamara was off for the day visiting her girlfriends. I had the day to explore Washington's churches. *Maybe alone, in one of these churches, I'll find my answers.*

At the corner of Wisconsin and Massachusetts Avenues was the Washington National Cathedral, an Episcopalian Church. Flying buttresses supported tall, stone walls of the massive neo-gothic structure, and big windows had sloping arches with pointed tops. *Is this place supposed to make you appreciate God? I feel so insignificant next to all of this. Go inside. Maybe there's more to it.* Inside, I swiveled my head to take in high vaulted ceilings, stone carvings, and colorfully stained-glass windows.

One trio of stained-glass windows depicted Moses as Prince of Egypt, with his staff before the Pharaoh, and with the Ten Commandments. Another stained glass window was dubbed, "Space Window," honoring the Moon landing, and included a lunar rock fragment. *Is this place honoring God, or man's attempt to search for God? I don't get it. Man getting to the moon was a pretty big achievement, but nothing that man does comes close to God's creation.*

Statues of George Washington and Abraham Lincoln stood as silent sentinels to America's history intertwined with religion. Two pairs of windows depicted the life of confederate Generals Robert E. Lee and Stonewall Jackson. *This cathedral memorializes people and events of great national significance. I get it. "In God we Trust." This sure is a grand place, but is God impressed by all of this? It just seems so empty.*

From there I visited the Shrine of the Immaculate Conception, a Roman Catholic Pilgrimage Church. I joined a tour. "Welcome to the Shrine of the Immaculate Conception. As the name implies, the Shrine is dedicated to the Blessed Virgin Mary. Now folks, before I go on, is everyone here Roman Catholic?" The seven of us in the tour nodded, glancing at one another. "Good, good. This is a special place. Come on in."

The long black robe of the priest giving the tour floated above the floor, as he strode, confident of the surroundings. The robe fell discreetly as he stopped to share his knowledge, "The Shrine was designed with both Byzantine and Romanesque architecture. The mosaic and marble throughout are distinctly Byzantine, whereas the stone sculptures of saints, sculpted archways, and the general shape of the church, are Roman. We're standing in the narthex, which is located between the nave and vestibule. The narthex, in early Christian architecture, was reserved for those who were not admitted amongst the congregation, so called penitents and catechumens."

Catechumens, the wannabe Catholics and the penitents, the sinners. Don't let them all the way in.

"Follow me, as we next enter the nave of the Shrine. Does anyone know the meaning of the word *nave*?"

An elderly gentleman at the front of the group raised his hand. "I believe the word nave is similar to the word 'naval,' as in *ship*." He spoke with a distinct New England accent.

"Correct, sir. The nave is the main open space for worship by those attending the church. The use of ship language is meant to relate to biblical stories such as that of Peter and the fishermen and Noah and his Ark. Now follow me just ahead to where the structure opens up side-to-side."

Again his robe flowed as he turned. "We call this area the *transept*. The transept spans the main axis of the church, making the church the shape of a Latin cross. The area in front of us is known as the upper church. The chancel of the upper church is reserved for the choir, deacons, and others assisting the priest in officiating the Mass. Past the chancel is the sanctuary, which contains (now for a term that many of you may not have heard of) the *Baldachin* altar. You see the canopy of columns and arches above the altar. The term *Baldachin* is related to the Spanish word *baldaquin* and the Italian word *baldacco* which refer to the lavishly brocaded material that was imported from Baghdad and hung over the altar.

"The vaulted, semicircle areas on either side of the sanctuary are known as the *apse*. Here in the North Apse is the mosaic entitled *Christ in Majesty*. It contains more than four thousand shades and colors."

Impressive, but is God impressed by it?

The tour group walked on. I stood contemplating the different terms that defined the structure and its contents. The numerous chapels within the Shrine were certainly ornate.

Fancy words. It's all so contrived, so high and mighty, but where is Christ in it? I want a connection with my Creator. The Shrine of the Immaculate Conception is just as empty as the National Cathedral.

I stopped for a quick lunch at the church cafeteria, and then was off again to downtown Washington, riding from one end of the city to the other along North Capital Street. The route took me past some rough, dirty looking areas in the Northeast sector before I eventually arrived at the Mall. The contrast between the street and the order and beauty of the Mall reminded me that America is a nation of contrasts: incredible wealth, but incredible poverty, awesome beauty, majesty and splendor, but a deep, dark, bloody, horrific history.

As I was leaving the Mall, I noticed a protest display calling for the government to find and bring home the Vietnam MIAs. One of the protestors was on a hunger strike and sitting in a small bamboo cage, to demonstrate the horror of soldiers missing in action. I stopped and signed the petition he demonstrated.

I left the Mall and found my way to the Arlington National Cemetery, where I visited John F. Kennedy's gravesite, the Tomb of the Unknown Soldier, and the monument of the Raising of the flag at Iwo Jima. I stood looking at the sea of white crosses neatly spaced on the well-manicured green grass. *These guys all died so young. They barely had a chance to live. Why do we have to have wars? Why do we have to kill each other? Why is the sacrifice for our freedom at the expense of all these young lives? How many hopes and dreams are entombed here?*

After Arlington I visited the Jefferson Monument and then headed to the Freer Museum. Oriental art was being showcased at the Freer. I saw drawings of tangled bodies enjoying sex. *The Japanese had their version of the Kama Sutra. Move along, there's no use getting hot and bothered alone in a museum.*

That night Tamara and I planned to see a movie at the National Air and Space Museum. We bought a simple bag lunch at a nearby grocery store and then hailed a cab for the museum. When we arrived, we discovered they were not showing movies this particular night, so we decided to walk on the Mall and view the lit-up monuments.

Washington took on an air of romance, as soft lights pierced the blackness to illuminate the hallowed sights. I was glad to have Tamara with me. I put my arm around her when the late

September night wind was chilly. I liked holding her close, and I wanted to kiss her. *Does she want me to kiss her? Not sure.*

We took the Washington Metro System back to 1626 Argonne. The Metro, or *Met* was a very clean, modern looking subway with no graffiti in sight. Luckily the subway trains were air-conditioned. Goose bumps danced on Tamara's bare arms. Once again I had an excuse to put my arm around her. She snuggled close to me, and my heart raced. We looked into one another's eyes and smiled.

I got to bed late, alone, around midnight.

The next morning John woke me early. I still felt tired. He made me a good breakfast, and, after a quick goodbye, I was on my way out of DC.

I tried to ride the bike path, but it wasn't always easy. In some areas, it followed the road and was very poorly marked. In other places the path ran through dreamy woods. Occasionally elevated wooden bikeways spanned marshland buzzing with life. Eventually I made my way to Mount Vernon where I toured the famous George Washington Mansion.

As I was going through the city of Arlington, I lost track of the bike route and then hit a sewer grate. My rear wheel sank into the grate with a forceful thrust, bending the rear derailleur, pushing it into the rear wheel spokes. I had to pull up hard on the bike to force it out of the sewer grate.

After examining the wheel and derailleur, I carefully pulled the derailleur away from the spokes. Holding the rear of the bike up, I spun the wheel and discovered it was true enough to ride. Within a few blocks, however, I heard the distinct hiss of a tire puncture. I pulled over and fixed the flat. Noisy traffic passed me. The air was warm and choking with exhaust. Frustration was welling up within me.

I paused and mentally reviewed the events of the past few days. I had warm memories of Washington: the monuments, memorials, the Mall, and the Churches, all of which combined to form an unexpectedly romantic setting. This was the back-drop of my meeting with Tamara. I hadn't kissed her despite a strong desire to do so. *Was the accident in the grate with the derailleur and the flat tire some sort of sign? Should I run toward the nearest pay phone and call Tamara, begging to see her again? I started this trip to look for answers, to look for God, not a girl.* God Bless America. The civil war was within me. *Just keep going, keep searching.*

V

A Ranger to the Rescue

¹⁷ Lord, how long wilt thou look on?
Rescue me from their destructions,
My precious life from the lions.
¹⁸ I will give You thanks in the great assembly:
I will praise You among many people.
Psalm 35:17-18 NKJV

At Dr. Mercer's Apothecary Shop in Colonial Fredericksburg, I learned that the doctor in those days acted not only as a general surgeon, but also as a pharmacist and dentist. Bottles of concoctions lined the old wooden shelves. Labels made various claims: some to heal, others to restore, and a few to expunge. Period actors recreated bloodletting and amputations that fascinated or horrified on-looking tourists. I stood intrigued, wanting more. Mary Washington's home, the Rising Sun Tavern, and James Munroe's Law Office, although interesting, paled in comparison to the history of the healing professions.

At the Presbyterian Church I learned that a nurse by the name of Clara Barton was the founder of the Red Cross. The church had been used as a war hospital during the civil war. I placed myself in the role of a long forgotten caregiver walking from bed to bed amongst moaning men with gaping wounds, burns, and mangled limbs.

The heat of the day penetrated my core as I began the noon-time ride. At times it felt too hot to cycle. I forced liquids into my body, pedaled on, and marveled once again at the relationships between the sweat dripping from my pores, water intake, physical effort, and the scorching sun.

My next stop was at George Washington's birthplace, now a designated National Historic Park. A young woman dressed in period costume stood in the doorway of the home. *Wow, she's cute, and that welcoming smile. She looks to be about my age.*

"Hi there," I said as I approached.

"Hello, and welcome to the childhood home of George Washington's birth. George was the first-born son of Augustine Washington and his wife Mary Ball Washington."

"I need a break from cycling in this heat."

"Come on in and look around. There's no air conditioning, but at least you'll be out of the sun."

"Thanks. Hey, how do you like working here?"

"I'm Susan, one of Mary Washington's housekeepers. My work here starts at dawn with milking the cows and ends at dusk with preparation of the Washington's evening meal."

She looked puzzled at the grin on my face.

"No, not that job. I mean working in period costume for the Park Service."

She giggled. "Not too many people ask me that. It's fun. We get to play different parts. Now it's not as busy as it gets during the summer months. There's lots of neat displays and reenactments. Take a look. You might enjoy."

"I will, thanks."

Along the bank of the Potomac, the Washington plantation was steeped in the history of slavery, indentured servitude, to-bacco trade with England, the Revolutionary War, and the first U.S. President. *I can't seem to concentrate on the history. Is there too much of it? Maybe it's the heat frying my brain. No, it's interesting, but it doesn't help me in my search. It doesn't stir me the way the history of healing does.*

I pushed my feet into the toe clips of the bicycle pedals and again felt the heat of the sun and now of the pavement below. It was like cycling in a sauna. My route along the road was in the direction of a gentle late summer breeze. This, coupled with my speed, made the hot air around me completely still. Wind was neither my friend nor foe.

After a long ride I came to Westmoreland State Park. The woodlands reminded me of Turkey Point Provincial Park back home. I rolled my bike toward the campground's shower and restroom building. Near heat exhaustion, I slowly dismounted. My head swam. I knew I had packed more cycling and sightseeing into this one particular day than I had before on this trip. I tried to revive myself with a can of soda from the machine outside of the building.

The *Coca Cola* was ice cold. I rolled it against my forehead and the nape of my neck. I pulled, and the can's tab gave a distinctive snap-click against the hot still air. I slowly sipped at the fizzy sweetness. Delicious, but not the cure for my state that I thought it would be.

A black van was parked outside of the shower building. In the men's room, as I splashed water on my face and neck, I could hear the carefree giggles of two young women on their side through the adjoining vaulted ceiling of the restrooms. Despite my fatigued state I drifted into a daydream amongst the giggles of these unknown women: a vivid display of one of these females making her way into the men's room to share a long, lathering, sensual shower with me.

Making a bowl with my cupped hands, I threw more water on my head. Massaging the water into my scalp I closed my eyes into the daydream. *Yeah, baby, how's that feel? Right there. Mmm. Oh yeah, that's the spot. Don't stop. Okay. Yeah, I want you too. Eyes open. More water. Colder water! Why am I torturing myself with this friggin' daydream? Snap out of it. The heat is getting to me. I'm spending too much time in wonderland.*

I made my way to a campsite beside another retired couple in an RV. As I unpacked and set up my tent, I wrestled with the decision whether to ease into my tent and drift into sleep or to nourish myself with a meal. The latter proved to be the necessity, no matter the effort. The tent was up, and I noticed the Park Ranger coming by in his truck to collect camp fees. I looked for my wallet in its normal resting place within the handlebar pack of the bicycle.

No wallet.

Where did I put it? I quickly looked through every pack and pocket I possessed. A memory: I had placed the wallet on the bicycle seat and then made my way into the men's restroom and shower. Those voices filtering over the wooden vaulted ceiling of the building, those voices that had become the point of a fantasy for my tired, yet hormone-raging body, those voices suddenly became a point of fear. They had picked up my wallet from its resting place.

The Park Ranger was a serious and official-looking man. He walked toward me with military precision. I studied his serious, chiseled face watching me from beneath his brimmed hat.

"That'll be eight dollars for your camp fee per night. You just here for the night?"

"I'm sorry, I know you're here for my camp fees, but I think I just lost my wallet."

He looked even more stern.

He thinks I'm attempting to freeload into a campsite. Quick, start explaining.

"I can pay you for the campsite. I have traveler's checks that I keep separate from my wallet." The checks were safely stowed inside the end of the handlebar tube. "When I first arrived here I rode my bike straight to the shower building. There was this black van. I think I left my wallet on the bike. Maybe someone from that van took it. Ya know, I could hear two women talking and giggling in the women's section." *Please believe me. Please help me out.*

The ranger's face again changed. The sternness was replaced by the look of a man with a mission. In an annoyed yet professional tone he said, "Wait here, I saw the van you just described as I drove in." As the ranger drove off in search of the black van I sat at the picnic table and whispered a silent prayer for the return of my wallet.

The ranger's truck rolled back toward my campsite twenty minutes later. He approached me with his same official sternness, and he produced my wallet. *They did take it.*

"Wow. You have no idea how happy I am to see that. Thank you. Thank you."

"You really need to be me more careful with this. I found the van parked at the beach parking lot, and the girls were still sitting there." There was pride in his voice. "Those girls first told me they never saw a bicycle or a wallet. So I pressed them with what a serious offense it is to steal within a patrolled campground. They kinda looked at each other uneasy like, so I knew something was up.

"They finally told me they found the wallet on the ground. Make sure that nothing's missing."

"Nothing appears to be missing, but it's been rifled through."

I handed the ranger my camp fees and waved to him as he drove away. Deep gratitude filled me. I continued unpacking in silence and meditative thanksgiving for my answered prayer.

The camp store and office were both closed for the season, eliminating the option of purchasing any food to prepare for dinner. I was too tired to mount the bicycle and ride out of the park to look for a store. The only foods I had with me were merely some Ritz Crackers and three-quarters of a pound of Colby cheese, mushy and moist from absorbing too much heat from the sun and the road.

My undergraduate Physical Education degree in physiology taught me without food my body would begin to break down — even break down the hard-earned muscle I'd gained up to this point in my tour. After cycling all day I needed filling and nutritious food to replenish and strengthen my body.

The delicious smells of the surrounding campsite meals drifted along to tease my nose as I sat snacking on cheese and crackers. I silently sent out another prayer, seeking food.

From the campsite behind mine a woman in her sixties walked toward me. "Excuse me, young man," she said. "There's four of us at our campsite and we've just finished eatin' and have a lot of food left over. We'll just be throwing it out unless you'd like some."

I assumed it was her husband from the campsite who said, "Leave the boy alone. He's traveling on his own and not looking for any handouts."

The woman rolled her eyes, ignoring the comment. I grinned in acknowledgement of her body language, "I'd love to have some of your leftovers. I didn't have time to supply myself with a meal, and only have some cheese and crackers."

Wow, God, thanks. That was fast.

She quickly turned back to her campsite and within minutes she returned with two chicken wings, two generously buttered rolls, and a large piece of chocolate cake.

"Thank you. You have no idea how much I appreciate this." I could feel the delicious food fuel my depleted body.

Is this the simple kindness of a stranger, or did God somehow intervene, or are both true somehow? Was the food really Your doing, God, or was it all by coincidence? Was that You orchestrating the return of my wallet, too? Doesn't matter. I'm thankful.

The long day ended in such peace that I slept with the tent fly off. The heavily wooded campsite cast a darkness sharply contrasting with the star-studded night sky. A chorus of singing insects disappeared as I slipped into sleep.

Waking early, I packed my tent before any other campers stirred. The land had an eerie feeling, blanketed by a dense, warm fog. The early morning ride of seven miles to Montross, Virginia spiked my hunger just in time for a good breakfast at the local diner.

The waitress glanced at my maps and bike helmet. "Ya got a pretty hot day for bike riding."

"I don't mind the heat, as long as I can keep drinking water and juice."

"Where ya coming from?"

"Yesterday I rode from Fredericksburg and stopped to camp at Westmoreland State Park. My trip started where I live in Canada." Her brown eyes widened, and her lips parted, as she tucked a strand of dark hair behind her ear.

"That's a long way to ride. Listen, honey, best you be careful out there. It's supposed to get up to ninety-five degrees today. I sure wouldn't wanna be out in that sweltering heat."

After breakfast I cycled down Highway 3, stopping only for fluids. The pavement radiated heat and combined with the hot sun and air. I felt as if I was trying to breathe with a plastic bag over my head.

Eventually Highway 3 led me to a very long bridge spanning the Rappahannock River between White Stone and Grey's Point, Highway 3 to Highway 33. *You made it Pat, way to go. Don't let the heat stop you. Now make it to 30.* Highway 30 to Highway 60. *Yes. I've got a lot of road behind me now. There's no head wind. Keep going, Pat. Yes, a sign for Williamsburg. Only ten miles more.*

Highway 646 brought me to the Williamsburg KOA Campground. I was tired, dehydrated, and again close to heat exhaustion. My feet felt worn out, and my ankles itched from numerous mosquito bites. *Yes, I did it. I knew I could.*

Crawling into my tent, I straightened my legs, which were on the verge of cramping. I reached over to my map and added up the mileage markers. One hundred and twenty miles. *Is that right?* I re-tallied the miles. *Yep, one hundred and twenty miles.* Goosebumps.

Crap! Hamstring cramp. Ouch. Stand. Can't stand. Rub. Straighten your leg. Straight. There. Oh crap, another cramp – the other leg. Get 'em both straight. Rub again. Drink water. Keep rubbing. Don't bend your knees. You're cramping because you over did it with the heat and distance. Just rest.

I needed a day of rest to recover.

VI
Chocolate, Baseball and Dad

¹¹ My son, do not despise the chastening of the LORD,
Nor detest His correction;
¹² For whom the LORD loves he corrects,
Just as a father the son in whom he delights.
¹³ Happy is the man who finds wisdom,
And the man who gains understanding;
¹⁴ For her proceeds are better than the profits of silver,
and her gain than fine gold.
Proverbs 3:11-14 NKJV

My next stop was in Colonial Williamsburg. I was content to resign myself to sightseeing instead of pounding the pedals for mile after mile. Numerous tourists saw me walk my bike, loaded with gear, and greeted me with encouraging smiles and warm introductions. One man was very interested in my trip, being an avid cyclist himself.

"Where you from?"

"Ontario, Canada."

"Did you ride all the way from there?"

"Yeah. I'm on my way to Florida."

"Florida. Wow! That's a ride. I do a lot of cycling myself; not today because I'm with my wife and kids, but what you're doing is remarkable."

"Thanks. Hey, do you know the area around here."

"We live nearby and visit the historic sites on weekends. It's a good way to teach the kids. What are you looking for?"

"I need a bike shop. I hit a sewer grate on my way out of DC, and my rear derailleur was badly bent."

"I know of a great shop, and it's close by." He quickly drew some directions on part of my Virginia map. "Here you go. I have to get back to my family. I wish you well on your journey."

"Thanks. It was good to meet you." We parted with a firm handshake. I watched him rejoin his wife, daughter, and son, and I could hear their questions as they walked away. "Where's he from? Where's he going?"

I stopped at McKenzie's Apothecary, one of the historic shops along the Duke of Gloucester Street in Colonial Williamsburg, and treated myself to a four-and-one-quarter ounce bar of "Fine Chocolate." The semisweet bar of chocolate melted in my mouth as I read the ingredients. The bars simple brown wrapper told the history of chocolate:

Chocolate, in cake form, was advertised and sold in Williamsburg by such eighteenth-century merchants as John Greenhow, Peter Hay, and John Carter. In the eighteenth century the chocolate was grated and added to milk to make a beverage, rather than being eaten as a confection as we do today. Hot chocolate was as fashionable a drink in colonial Virginia as coffee or tea. The ingredients used for this semi-sweet chocolate bar are basically the same as those used in the eighteenth century. The shape of the bar is modern.

Two dollars is a lot of money to spend on a chocolate bar. I walked away from the apothecary satisfied, though, reveling in the bar's thick, musky, sweet taste, and thinking I'd spent two dollars wisely.

Bruton Parish Church drew my attention as I walked my bicycle along. I picked up the guide to the church and learned it was Episcopalian. The stately five-hundred-seat church had undergone many changes in its history, but had been in continuous use since 1715. I read its *Architectural Notes*, stating its cross-shaped foundation had been created "less from religious symbolism than from a desire to accommodate college and government personnel during special times."

The church was made of warm, old, oiled wood. I stopped and contemplated the High Box Pews, craftily designed to keep illustrious parishioners such as Washington, Jefferson, Munroe, and Tyler warm during cold winter Sundays.

Church and state were not separate in Colonial Virginia. In fact, anyone holding political office was obliged by law to attend church regularly. Interestingly, two Episcopalians, George Mason and James Madison, drafted the provision for religious toleration in the 1776 Declaration, which paved the way for church disestablishment. *Perhaps these guys wanted to sleep in on the occasional Sunday.*

The Burton Parish Church had a simplicity that was in sharp contrast to the Washington National Cathedral and the Roman Catholic Shrine of the Immaculate Conception. *It doesn't feel like God is in here either, though. I need to connect with you, Lord. Where are you?* I walked out of the church.

I did not purchase any tickets to view reenactments such as the jeweler bending metal and setting stones, the blacksmith pounding metal into useful shapes, or the coppersmith crafting vessels. I was simply content to see the town, its architecture and trees, and drink in its old world ambiance.

The Colonial Parkway led me from Williamsburg to Jamestown. The peaceful nine-mile stretch of road was lined in lush green. I pulled into the Jamestown Beach Campsite-Resort where I registered.

I took a picture of the old Anglican Church. Built in 1639, it was the first brick church, built to replace the first place of worship at Jamestown, a simple tent made from old sailcloth. Reverend Robert Hunt was the first priest, sent by the Church of England along with the first settlers. He had been responsible for the welfare of the brave souls venturing to the English Colony of Virginia.

Hunt's efforts helped establish the Anglican Church that – over the years – transformed from sailcloth to timber, and then to brick. Within the walls of the timber church, in the spring of 1614, it is believed that John Rolfe was wed to Pocahontas, the daughter of Chief Powhatan.

Was it a marriage of political convenience created by John Rolfe and Chief Powhatan? How did the other colonists view their marriage? Did John Rolfe really love Pocahontas? Did he and she have a spiritual connection in their marriage, and, if so, did any notion of their connection rest in the religious ceremony and vows in the church?

I walked toward the simple bronze statue of Pocahontas. The metal statue was oxidized green, making her appear to be stepping out of the surrounding trees. The sculptor had immortalized her with an earthly beauty, softness, grace, and poise. If she was anything close to her immortalized statue, then John Rolfe had chosen a lovely bride.

The very same church served as the meeting site of the first representative legislative assembly in the American English Colony. The 1619 meeting heralded independence by establishing self-government for all of the colonies. As my tour of Jamestown wound to an end, I contemplated America's penchant for immortalizing anything that was a first in her history.

One of the Jamestown Park Rangers gave me a list of names to scan to determine if Milroy, or any of their related surnames, were amongst the first settlers. According to the information sheet I received, there were one-hundred-forty-four persons in the expedition. There was no Milroy.

Sights and sounds of the Jamestown Scottish Festival drew me to Jamestown Festival Park, located near the campground. I paid the five-dollar admission fee, despite the fact that the day's activities were coming to an end. *Dad would have really enjoyed the bag pipers if he were with me.* As a child, the sound of bagpipes would make me cringe. On this day, though, they filled me with excitement, and gooseflesh spread across my body.

I came across a table set up with information on Scottish Tartans. I ran my fingers across the tartan of MacGillivray Clan, of which Milroy was a Sept, or sub clan. My throat tightened. *Dad would have loved this Scottish Festival. I wish he was here with me.* The emotions welling up in me were mixed. Dad had worked hard over the years, climbed the corporate ladder striving ever to improve his earnings in support of his wife and six children, needing to exert his natural born ability to lead, while at the same time he sought an escape from the constraints of family life.

Two young boys playing catch drew my attention away from the festival. I watched their singular focus as they tracked the ball into their mitts.

When I was nine and ten I had played little league baseball. My maternal grandfather was a great fan. I did not play ball out of pure love for the game. Instead, in my nine-year old mind, baseball created an opportunity for me to be closer to my Dad. I watched in envy as the other boys in our neighborhood played catch in the evenings with their fathers. Dad was out of the house and on his way to work before I was awake and he was home late in the evening after I went to bed. On the occasional day when he was home early, I did not understand the level of fatigue that caused him to slump in his favorite easy chair.

"Dad, come and play catch with me."

I was a long, lanky, uncoordinated, daydreaming, nine-year old boy. I now look back and feel sorry for the coaches who were charged with teaching me the game and slotting me into a field position that did the least damage to the team's chances of winning. I was invariably put in the outfield. The coaches, much like me, hoped the ball would never be hit my way; but of course, it was.

I was paralyzed with the fear of being hit, by my inability to read the trajectory of the ball, and by not knowing where to throw it. It would either fly over my head or bounce in front of me. On the rare occasion when it hit my glove, there was a glimmer of hope in my team that Milroy had finally caught a fly ball. It was not to be. I had not mastered the skill of allowing the ball to land firmly in the pocket of my glove before closing the leather around it. The ball would bounce to the ground. I would pick it up and make a lazy, weak-armed, looping throw toward the infield that allowed even the slowest of runners to make his base safely.

"Easy out, easy out, hey, batter, batter, swing!" I rarely swung at the ball. Standing in the batter's box I would take a couple of practice swings. One of my coaches would yell, "Milroy, don't step in the bucket." Invariably, I stepped in the bucket, not understanding their terminology for proper foot-work in the batter's box.

During my second season of playing in Shoreview, Minnesota, I actually did make contact with the ball. I stood in the batter's box and carefully watched the first two pitches hurled at me. One was called a ball and the other a strike. At the top of the pitcher's wind-up, I closed my eyes and swung at what I thought would be the right time for the ball to be over the plate.

I opened my eyes in shock and dismay when the impact of the hard ball sent vibrations into the bat that hurt my fingers. The ball popped up with a fast spin to the pitcher. I began running in what felt like slow motion toward first base. "Run, Milroy," my coach screamed. I was halfway down the first base line when I saw the pitcher take two easy strides and catch the ball.

As I returned to the bench in disappointment, I was in a state of confusion, as every member of my team came forward to congratulate me. My coach took me aside and rubbed my still stinging hands.

"There, you see, Pat, you made contact. You can do it."

"Yeah, Coach, but I closed my eyes when I swung." I walked away feeling my Coach's bewilderment and disappointment.

During another game I was up to bat, and again the first two pitches screamed through to the catcher. Both pitches were called balls. My mantra when I was up to bat was "Walk me. Walk me. Please walk me."

I was deep into my mantra and staring not at the pitcher and the ball, but somewhere out into right center field, lost in thought, when a screaming fastball hit me square in the left kidney region. A collective *"Ohhhh"* and sigh came from my bench and the parents of both teams watching the game. I doubled over from the searing pain. The impact caused me to lose my breath. The bat dropped from my hand.

The umpire stepped from behind home plate and began to rub my side, gently but firmly. Tears leapt from my eyes. I tried to run from the umpire's grasp toward my painfully awarded first base.

"Take it easy, son," the umpire said, holding me back. "Why didn't you get out of the way of that pitch?"

I looked back at him and said, "I just wanted to get on base."

"Listen kid, there's a lot of easier ways to get on base than that."

I shook myself from his grasp and said, "Not for me," as I staggered up the first base line to the obligatory applause given to the injured as the game resumed.

Playing baseball was my attempt to force my dad into spending time with me. As a kid I did not understand the enormous pressures my father endured to support our family, improve our lifestyle, and quench his own ambitions.

I was sorry to hear the last of the bag pipers playing as the band marched off the Jamestown Festival Ground to a steady, subduing drumbeat.

Back at the Jamestown Beach Campground, I listened to the sounds around me: crickets chirping, the whir of winged insects, dogs barking at other campsites, and the muffled voices of surrounding campers. The dark woods were peaceful, and I fell asleep.

VII
The Forest Tabernacle

7 Moses took his tent and pitched it outside the camp, far from the camp, and called it the tabernacle of meeting. And it came to pass that everyone who sought the Lord went out to the tabernacle of meeting which was outside the camp.
Exodus 33:7 NKJV

A light rain fell on the forested campground early in the morning of September twenty-eight. I awoke with the morning rain, packed my tent and left the campground by seven o'clock. The town of Jamestown was quiet and still. I rolled my bike to a stop and stood straddling the bike and leaning on the handlebars, looking up and down the street. I was alone. None of the quaint looking shops were open. I hesitated, but not because of any overt danger. Rather, it was a gut instinct that I could not identify. *What is it? What am I to do?* My whispers were met with an irksome silence.

I rechecked my maps and pushed off, coasting down the main street. It was a short ride to the ferry that crosses the James River to a small town called Scotland, Virginia.

As I waited on the dock, standing next to my trusty well-laden steed, two young women pulled up in a VW Bug and parked behind my bike. They approached me with a tentative curiosity, smiling as they introduced themselves. Jessica and Rachel listened to the description of my trip, and we talked of travel in general.

Jessica said, "Yes, it really is easy to lose track of time when you travel."

"By the way, what day is it?" I asked.

"It's Sunday," they replied in unison. "We're on our way to Church on the other side of the river."

"Sunday. I thought it was only Saturday." I continued in conversation with them, learning of a restaurant for breakfast not far from the town of Scotland. The girls climbed back into their car and drove onto the ferry. I pushed my bike onto the ferry and secured it for the short voyage across the river.

Traveling by bicycle with goals such as towns to visit and states to be covered had caused days to slip by. I was not aware it was Sunday. I had visited and immersed myself in many churches along my way, but I had not attended a church service of any kind since I began my trip.

As the ferry pulled into the river, Jessica approached me again, "Pat, Rachel and I are going to have breakfast on the other side of the river, and I was wondering if you would like to join us? But before you answer, please understand that the breakfast is being held at a Retreat Centre and today is the last day of the retreat. It's put on by our local Church."

"I grew up Catholic, and so I've been to retreats before. As for breakfast, I can get pretty hungry riding this bike. Thank you. Yeah. Sure. I'd like to join you for breakfast."

Jessica's instructions from the ferry landing took me through a short uphill climb and a couple of turns onto a secluded country road. The Retreat Center was nestled in thick woodland, overlooking the James River. I leaned my bicycle against the side of the unassuming, square, white building.

The breakfast consisted of pancakes smothered in blueberries, plus grits and orange juice. I had my first-time-ever bites of grits and swallowed my last bite thinking they were kind of boring, although, they do fill you up.

Notwithstanding the grits, the meal was as wholesome and filling as the company surrounding me. I felt a sense of obligation to attend the service that was to follow breakfast and accepted their invitation. *Am I looking for an invitation to share in their worship? Was God's hand in the early morning meeting with Jessica and Rachel leading me to this retreat center?*

A Roman Catholic priest from Arizona led the worship service. The Priest read the gospel and then gave a sermon on what it really means to be poor in spirit. The sermon hit me hard, as my own spiritual dilemma caused me to identify with his description. He explained that in our American material society the acceptance of poverty is nearly impossible. He described the refugees, the elderly, and those on fixed incomes whom he saw as being materially poor. He said the materially poor were often richest in spirit because of their simple yet strong faith in God and Christ as their Savior.

Sitting at the service, I renewed my belief in my Creator. My spiritual dilemma deepened as I realized my belief in Christ as my Savior was shaky at best. *Where's the simple childlike faith I grew up with? As a kid, I had loved Christ.*

The service had all the earmarks of the familiar Roman Catholic Mass, including the celebration of the Eucharist. At Holy Communion everyone stood in a circle to receive the Eucharist. I sat back in my front row seat. Rachel stepped away from the circle of people, walked over to me, and quietly sat in the chair next to me. Leaning toward me, she whispered, "Pat, you are welcome to join us for the Eucharist."

"Thanks, Rachel, I can't. It's hard to explain, but I feel like an observer here and not a participant." Rachel's demeanor changed slightly, and I was immediately compelled to explain. "All of you have been so kind and welcoming to me. I just have a lot of confusion regarding my spirituality and it's preventing me from joining in."

Rachel touched my hand. "That's okay, Pat." She returned to the circle. The Priest continued with his Mass. The people in the circle were holding hands and swaying together in what was clearly meditation. I sat observing, content in feeling fully accepted by these friendly, caring people, who wiped away any thought that I might be intruding on their retreat.

Jessica and Rachel had introduced me to a young married couple, Patricia and her husband Pat, at breakfast. Everyone laughed when I said, "Well, that's easy for me to remember!" At Mass, the two of them were standing directly in front of me in the circle. They loosened their hands from one another, made a half turn toward me, and looked at me with inviting smiles. In perfect unison they motioned for me to join them and partake in the Eucharist. My head began to swim, and time seemed to slow down. The circle of people before me beckoned me to join them. The rest of the room seemed to melt away.

My brow furrowed with confusion. I could feel my throat tighten. *Don't do it, stay seated. You'd be a hypocrite to join them.* I shook my head slowly, declining yet another invitation to partake in the Eucharist.

"Okay, Pat. No pressure." They returned to the circle.

My mind whirled with questions as I watched blankly. *Am I just being plain stubborn? How coincidental must an incident be before I accept it as God trying to influence or reach me? Had God arranged my meeting Rachel and Jessica today so that I might hear His word and see His love through The Priest and the other participants at the retreat center?*

The Eucharist Celebration of the service ended, and the people in the circle dispersed to their chairs for quiet reflection. The Priest then announced a forty-five-minute break for quiet reflection. Many of the participants reverently stood up and walked out of the building into the late morning sunshine.

The priest walked toward me and I stood. Jessica and Rachel also approached along with another man. "Pat, I want you to meet our Minister." Jessica motioned toward the other man whose name sounded so different that it didn't register with me. I put my hand out to shake his, but he mumbled something and turned away. I could feel a darkness about him, something creepy.

"Never mind him, Pat. He's having a bad day," said the Priest.

"Father, I'm sorry I couldn't join the communion; I was raised in this stuff, but I'm too confused in my belief. I feel as if I am an observer."

The Priest put his hand on my shoulder, smiled and said, "Pat, why don't you take a few minutes to walk down one of the trails here. They are beautiful, and you can clear your head."

"Thanks, Father. I will." We shook hands. Turning, I spotted Rachel and Jessica.

"Breakfast was great. Thanks for inviting me. I'll be leaving the retreat center after I take a walk through the woods."

They smiled again and wished me well on the rest of my bicycle tour.

Walking into the now warm sunshine, I chose a path across the dirt parking area in front of the retreat center entrance. The trail through the woods led along a steep hilltop with the James River below. Lofty trees surrounded me, and a warm pine-needle scent filled my nostrils as I wandered down the trail. The peace and quiet of the woods helped to calm the turmoil of my mind.

Walking into an empty church, I had sometimes felt the same peace and quiet. *Was the peace and quiet simply because the world's hustle and bustle remained on the outside? Or was it because of the presence of God?*

The Roman Catholic Church attempted to possess the presence of God through the use of the tabernacle, which houses the Eucharist. The Catechism of the Catholic Church teaches that in its churches throughout the world the "tabernacle should be located in an especially worthy place in the church and should be constructed in such a way that it emphasizes and manifests the truth of the real presence of Christ in the Blessed Sacrament."

The Old Testament tabernacle was at first a tent that served as a place of worship for the Israelites. Then God told Moses to build a permanent tabernacle as a center for worship. Israelites believed that the Ark of the Covenant was the most holy structure. It was the only piece of furniture in the innermost room, or *Holy of Holy's*, of the tabernacle. The *Ark*, the resting place of God, was covered with a golden lid known as the *Mercy Seat*. Gold Cherubim adorned both ends of the *Mercy Seat*. The Israelites believed that on the Day of Atonement God would speak to the high priest. The *Mercy Seat* was sprinkled with sacrificial blood as atonement for man's sin.

I came upon a small clearing to my left along the trail. In among the trees were simple benches made from tree stumps and wooden planks that appeared to be cut from the trees felled to clear the area. The benches stood in front of a large, simple wooden cross. Behind the cross were more trees, and the land dropped sharply down toward the James River below. On the cross, draped around the top beam, was a simple wreath of thorns. I stood on the path looking at the cross. Peace, quiet, and solitude engulfed me.

My legs weakened as I stepped into this cathedral in and of the woods. I held my gaze on the cross and the thorns.

The cross. The crown of thorns. You suffered because of me. You died for me. You love me. My eyes filled with tears. There in the Virginia woods, above the James River, with the day's sunshine filtering through the surrounding pine trees I was no longer alone.

I was in the presence of Jesus Christ.

The most beautiful white light that I could not just see, but feel throughout the core of my body, radiated from Him as he stood close to my right side. Love: pure, complete, infinite love emanated from Jesus.

Hot burning tears streamed down my face. As quickly as I had the thought that I should be on my knees before Christ, His loving voice, a voice as soft as a rose petal, a voice as sweet as honey, and a voice as powerful as the ocean, said, "Pat, just sit and rest." I sat on one of the benches.

"Pat, you've been looking for Me."

"Yes."

"I'm right here." His presence was undeniable. Burning tears kept pouring from my eyes. "Pat, I love you." His love continued to radiate through me.

"Pat, something is going to happen to you. I wish I could stop it, but this is a fallen world."

"What's going to happen to me? Will I be killed? Will I be injured?"

"You will not be killed or injured. But something terrible will happen to you. I want you to follow Me. I love you."

"How can I follow You? I don't even know if I believe in You. I can handle whatever happens to me."

"Pat, I don't want this to happen to you."

"No. I can't believe in You," I sat, shaking my head, as tears continued to flow in a steady stream down my cheeks.

I feared that if I was to follow Christ, I would be asked by Him to enter the Catholic priesthood. This was my childhood understanding of "being called by Christ." It meant I would be alone, alone as in without a mate. At that time in my life I could not visualize a calling by Christ outside of the church.

"Pat, I love you."

"But I can't believe in You."

"I love you anyway, always."

"I have to live my life my way." My mind knew I was speaking to a very real person in Jesus Christ, yet I continued to deny Him.

In a powerful, loving voice, Christ said, "The path you are choosing will be a difficult one."

"I don't care. This is my life and my path."

"Pat, I love you, and I do not want to see you suffer."

"I need to live my life my way."

"Pat, I love you, and I will walk with you anyway."

"I have to choose my own path in life."

"I love you anyway."

I turned from Christ's presence and noticed the front of my shirt was tear-soaked. I wiped the thick salty tears from my eyes, slowly stood, and walked out of the Forest Tabernacle. The deep content I felt in deciding to live my life on my terms and not with Christ was tempered with a profound sense of loss. I walked along the trail back toward the retreat center and opened the door, only to find the center was empty. I slowly mounted my bicycle and rode away.

What just happened? Did I really just meet Jesus? It was real. That was Jesus, and I just turned from Him.

My sense of spirituality had been married so tightly to the Catholic Church that I felt little distinction between the Church and a relationship with Christ. Much of my identity had been defined by the strict traditional Roman Catholic culture imposed upon me as a child. *Why do I take this religion and spirituality so seriously? Most of my friends don't.*

I had allowed my crisis of faith to undermine relationships in my life. In stubborn and selfish anger I had turned away from my parents and my fiancé Gerda in the same way I had turned away from the Catholic Church. I had caused much pain in her life. As I pedaled, my thoughts drifted back to our relationship.

Witnessing Gerda's personal relationship with Christ was a major influence in my questioning of, and letting go of my faith in the Catholic Church.

I had attended a few meetings for Christians at the university. At some of the meetings we were asked to answer some basic questions regarding Christian faith. My answers rolled off my pen like childhood catechism, by rote. I found those answers empty at the time, even though they more than satisfied the Christians attending the meetings.

Because my relationship with Christ had never been made personal within the Catholic Church, I felt a huge disconnect from the relationship that the attendees of those meetings espoused. I didn't know what such a relationship would mean. I suspected that a personal relationship with Him would be far better than the ritualistic, dogmatic relationship of the Catholic Church. It was a gulf I had to work out for myself. Letting go of my Catholicism was the only way I thought I could find the truth about having a personal relationship with Christ.

In my "good Catholic boy" persona I had given Gerda an ultimatum. She was to become a Roman Catholic if we were to marry. *Who the hell did I think I was to do that to her?* I had become her sponsor at the catechumen classes. She listened intently and weighed her Dutch Reformed Church beliefs against those of Roman Catholicism. Some of the teachings she easily accepted. Some she admitted having difficulty with.

As her catechumen sponsor, I was to assist her in becoming the proverbial "good catholic girl." With each class I had grown more discontented. I had asked more questions in the classes than any of the catechumens. The priests and nuns responded to my questions with rote catechism answers that left me unsatisfied and frustrated.

Gerda had become a Catholic for me, but my ever-growing list of questions led to a deep discontent too difficult for me to sort out. I tried to explain my frustration to Gerda, but to no avail. Her relationship with Christ was genuine, and the place of worship was seemingly irrelevant. The church she attended was only a vehicle for her spirituality. Her relationship with Christ was personal, real, and independent of any Church.

The Catholic Church and Christ had been inseparable during my youth. I had loved the Christ of the Church with its First Confession, First Communion, and Confirmation.

My parents and the Church had done a great job indoctrinating me. As an infant I was baptized into the Church without my knowledge or consent. *Take your sins to a priest; he has the ear of Christ.* The ritual of the Eucharist was where good Catholics held communion with Christ. *You sinned? No communion for you until you enter the secrecy and sanctity of the confessional to tell your priest the sin and ask for forgiveness.* The priest controlled my connection with Christ. There was little room for a personal relationship with Christ. The Church had it all.

Angry and confused, I walked away from the church. My childhood relationship with Christ had been so tightly knit to the Roman Catholic Church that a personal relationship with Christ was now impossible for me.

I could easily blame the Roman Catholic Church for my turning from Christ at the Forest Tabernacle. However, the choice was much deeper and more powerful than any blame I could heap onto any Church. Sure, the Catholic Church has a long history of ritualizing and institutionalizing the most sacred part of our existence, our personal relationship with our Creator and Savior, but that did not figure into my choice.

[13] Who is wise and understanding among you? Let him show by good conduct that his works are done in the meekness of wisdom. [14] But if you have bitter envy and self-seeking in your hearts, do not boast and lie against the truth. [15] This wisdom does not descend from above, but is earthly, sensual, demonic. [16] For where envy and self-seeking exist, confusion and every evil thing are there. [17] But the wisdom that is from above is first pure, then peaceable, gentle, willing to yield, full of mercy and good fruits, without partiality and without hypocrisy. *James 3:13-17 NKJV*

The real reason I turned from Christ rested squarely on my own shoulders. I was self-centered, self-sufficient and self-indulgent. I was selfish. It was a turning point in my life, when I believe I could manage life better through my will than the will of the One who created the universe.

The fact that I had met Christ in the woods, away from the Roman Catholic Tabernacle, was of little consolation for me. Finally, my relationship to Christ was real, but I had just said "no" to that relationship.

VIII
Canaan's Campground

[11] Then Lot chose for himself all the plain of Jordan, and Lot journeyed east. And they separated from each other. [12] Abram dwelt in the land of Canaan, and Lot dwelt in the cities of the plain and pitched *his* tent even as far as Sodom. [13] But the men of Sodom *were* exceedingly wicked and sinful against the Lord.
Genesis 13:11-13 NKJV

The weather changed. The warm sunshine that had filtered through the trees of the Forest Tabernacle was replaced by a stiff headwind. Dark pillows of cloud cast shadows that I rode in and out of. *The changing weather seems to match the change in my spiritual direction, turmoil, yep, but it's my turmoil.*

My goal for the day was to ride to Virginia Beach, Virginia. I battled a stiff wind. The effort of each pedal stroke, coupled with the morning's emotions and my encounter with Christ, found me quickly exhausted. My legs felt as if they were filled with lead, and I needed sleep. I rode as far as Suffolk, Virginia, and pitched my tent at Sleepy Hole Park.

Sixteen-year old Jenny stood behind the camp registration counter. She watched as I wrote my home address on the registration card. She looked out the window at my bike and then back at me standing with my helmet under my arm, her hazel eyes widening.

"Did you ride your bike all the way here from Canada?"

"Yeah, I did."

"Wow. I never did meet someone who'd done somethin' like that before. Hey, Billy!"

Jenny's older brother was at the other end of the registration counter. "Jenn, mind your bus'ness. I don't give a hoot what he did."

"You ain't done anything like that. You're jus' jealous."

"Shut up, Jenn, or I'll shut you up." Billy stormed out the back door of the camp office.

"Never mind him. I think what your doin's pretty neat. I'd like to get away from here some day."

She's not happy about something here. Her brother seems like a real jerk. "Maybe you will. You just have to make up your mind and then go do it."

"You're right, maybe someday. Nice to meet you, Pat from Canada. The campground is pretty empty. You can pitch your tent anywhere."

About fifty yards from the campground shower and bathroom outbuilding, I pitched my tent between a line of towering conifers with the tent opening facing a large open field.

Roy and Marie Pennington had their massive RV parked at a site across the camp road but close to mine. Marie's demeanor was a mixture of southern belle and matronly charm. Long lashes and olive skin defied her retirement age and accented her dark brown eyes. Roy was a tall man, completely grey-haired, with shiny blue eyes, and thick, large calloused blue-collar hands. He walked with a "just got off a horse" stiffness that showed his age.

They listened intently as I explained my tour to date, giving highlights such as crossing the border at Niagara Falls, the steepness of the Allegany Mountain passes in Pennsylvania, and visiting Washington, DC.

"Where will you be heading to from here?" Marie's tone was motherly.

"I wanted to get to Virginia Beach today, but the strong wind slowed me down. I got a late start because of a pancake breakfast in Scotland. I'll head for Virginia Beach tomorrow."

Marie's face furrowed, showing her wrinkles. Roy tipped his head forward and slowly turned it side to side in deep concern. They knew the area. They knew the traffic patterns and the road conditions.

"Pat," Roy said. "We'll put your bike in our RV and drive you to Virginia Beach. The highway you have to travel on is way too dangerous for a bicycle, and besides you are talking about riding in the Monday morning traffic."

Marie said, "Pat, we fear for your safety."

"Thanks, but I made up my mind to ride my bicycle all of the way. Putting my bike in your RV just doesn't seem right."

Roy and Marie looked at one another with the parental concern that one has when teaching a child to look both ways before crossing the street. "We insist, Pat. It's just too dangerous," Marie said.

"Okay," I replied, with a sense of defeat and yet comfort in their company.

"We were planning on an early start, Pat, so we're not in rush hour traffic. Can you be awake by 4:30 a.m.?"

"I sure can, Roy, but I have no alarm, so just come near my tent and give me a good morning 'hello.'" We shook hands and went into our respective dwellings for the night.

I lay awake in my tent. I was not lonely, but I felt alone in the world. For the first time on the trip I felt the hardness and harshness of the ground underneath my tent. The night air was warm, but there was a blackness and coldness that felt like a void.

I reviewed the day: *Jessica and Rachel, The Priest, my visit with Christ, the strange shift in the weather and finally the kindness of Roy and Marie.* I felt a pang of disappointment and guilt as I realized the compromise I had made in my journey by accepting their offer.

I closed my eyes and felt my own autonomy in this world. I quietly confirmed my independence from my childhood faith in Christ and the boundaries set forth by the religion of my birth, Roman Catholicism. Indeed, I would determine for myself what was right and what was wrong. I had set out to redefine my own ethical code and to act morally, based upon that code.

I had not put the fly on my tent. I looked out into blackness. There was such a stillness and quiet about the earth that I could no longer make out trees. Once again exhausted from hard cycling, I drifted into sleep.

The sound of my tent zipper opening stirred me. "Pat. Pat." Someone was whispering as I began to stir. *Someone's here to visit me.*

Suddenly, my ankles were grabbed by two strong hands and in one swift pull, I was hauled out of my tent.

"Who? What? What are you doing? Stop! No! Let me go!" I tried to kick away from the strong grasp, flailing my arms.

"Watch his legs. He's strong. Hold him. Cover his face."

Total fear engulfed me. I struggled against the men holding me. *What's happening? No! Somebody help me.* My face was quickly covered with a cloth that was held firm by one of their hands. I struggled, trying to breathe. *Can't breathe. Blackness.* My body was completely limp. *I'm being carried. More blackness. It feels like I'm floating. What is happening?*

I came to in a room, naked. My senses blunted. The surface I was lying on was hard, like an old oak floor. As I sat up I had trouble focusing to see. Two men were in the room, standing in a dark corner. My head swam with fatigue coupled with whatever drug they had used on me.

"Stand up." The firm voice came from the corner.

I staggered to my feet and stood with my hands covering my genitals. "Where am I? Who are you? Why am I here?"

"I'll ask the questions. Why are you covering yourself up? Are you ashamed of your body? You've got nothin' we haven't seen before. Put your hands down so we can see your dick."

"Let me go. Why are you doing this?"

"Put your hands down, and show us your dick, or we'll do it for you."

I clenched my fists at my sides.

"What do you think you're gonna do with that little dick? You don't have a hope in hell of pleasuring a woman."

"Why are you doing this?" My head swam as I stood facing them.

"We're going to *fuck* your pretty ass. You can participate and make this a lot easier on yourself."

"Participate? What are you talking about? Show yourself, you fucking cowards. I'll fight you. I'll never participate. Let me go."

"You're in no condition to fight. You can barely stand, and you're not going anywhere." He laughed. His laugh was sinister, conniving and dismissive of me as a person. I was just a piece of meat for them to do with – whatever they wanted. "There's no way out of here. Besides, what are you going to do, run down the street naked? You don't even know where we've taken you. Don't be a fool. You're ours."

"I know who you are. You better let me go."

He addressed the other man in the shadow with him. "He thinks he knows who I am." Then said to me, "Who the hell do you think I am?"

"You're that priest from the retreat center. I know your voice."

"I guess he does know who I am. Okay, we'll just have to kill him when we're done fucking him."

"Let me go. You'll never get away with killing me. You're supposed to be a good person. You're a priest. Why are you doing this?"

"Never mind why. I'm going to fuck you, kill you, and then burn you in a furnace. No one knows where you are. You've got no choice in the matter. You can participate, or we'll drug you. Either way we're fucking your ass all night long."

I was struck by my complete state of helplessness. *Are they going to kill me when they're done with me? I don't want to die.* "You better drug me, cause I'll never participate, but don't kill me. Please, I don't want to die. I won't tell anyone."

"We'll see about not killing you."

"Please, no, I don't want to die."

The other man motioned me forward with a wave of his hand. I sat in a wooden chair while he injected something into my arm. Blackness ensued.

I was engulfed by a presence. My body was held in a state of levitation. My ankles and wrists were held by cold, insensitive, powerful claw-like appendages that extended from a Demon Beast. I struggled against the cold greasy metal-like grasp of the Demon Beast in futility. The Demon Beast laughed at me and said, "You can't fight me."

The Demon Beast's black wings were like that of a rotting carcass, taut and putrefied. "No one is here to help you."

I tried to shout *"help!"* but the Demon Beast drew me against his body with such a suffocating force that my cries for help could not be heard. I turned my head from the Demon Beast, *No. No. Let me go.*

The demon beast laughed again, mockingly. I writhed as I tightened my buttocks and pulled away from him. I continued to struggle and plead until deep within me I knew I needed the help of my Savior Jesus.

"Jesus," I gasped through the suffocation.

The Demon Beast laughed with cold, heartless, evil. "Your Jesus can't help you. Remember, you turned away from Him. You're under my control now."

Exhausted and drugged, I could no longer fight. He tightened his grip on me, hovering and holding my legs up and out, and my arms up and out, as I was repeatedly sodomized. *No. No! Stop, please stop, no! Someone help me.* I thought the terror would never end. This was a state of complete and utter helplessness. *Stop. Please stop! No. Stop!* The thrusts wounded my very being.

I came to during the violation. I was restrained at my wrists and ankles, on a bondage table, as the perpetrator thrust himself into me.

"I think he's wakin' up. Hey look, I think he likes it, he's got a boner." The voice came from the stranger standing at my head.

"He don't like it. It's just a reflex 'cause I'm screwing his pretty ass."

"He won't remember us, will he?"

"Hold his head up." The stranger at my head pulled hard on my hair and held my head so that I could face the perpetrator. "Hey, boy, if you can hear me, keep your mouth shut about this or we'll kill you. You got that? We'll kill you."

No. Don't kill me. I want to live. Please, don't kill me. I couldn't speak. I knew that my head was being held up, but in my drugged haze I could only see the dark shapes of the men violating me. On the other hand, I could feel everything. One man was huge, with thrusts that hurt. The other man was smaller.

"Put him under again." I fell back into the blackness again. The Demon Beast continued to thrust into me.

In defiance to the Demon Beast, and through the suffocation I cried out, "Jesus, Jesus, Jesus."

"He's not here."

"Jesus, Jesus, Jesus."

I saw a small flicker of light. The thrusts stopped. The Demon Beast released his grasp.

I came to again briefly, and heard the voices of my tormentors.

"He's had enough. We don't want a corpse."

"We're done with him. Clean him up." Again, I fell into blackness.

I was being carried. Voices murmured. *I'm floating again. I'm falling. Help.*

The ground was hard when I landed. Blackness. Terrified, I curled into the fetal position in my tent. My chest heaved as I drew in air. The cold of the ground contrasted with the warmth of the night air. *Don't sleep, Pat. Don't sleep. The terror will return.* I searched through the darkness looking for a sign of safety and security. There was nothing. Too terrified to leave my tent, exhausted, I slipped in and out of light sleep. The terror of the night was not over. Vivid visions haunted me.

In the first vision, I was sitting at a desk, surrounded by books piled high around me. I drank information from the book before me. The message was clear. I would continue studying. Studying for me was never easy. Retaining information was always a struggle, causing me to study more intently and for longer times than my peers. I had an overriding sense of dread about the sheer volume of information that I was to learn.

The Demon Beast said, "What are you going to try to prove by learning? You're nothing. You'll fail. You'll never make a difference."

I will learn anyway. You can't stop me. I moaned in my sleep, tossing.

The second vision was more vivid and powerful than the first. This was of the woman I would marry and attempt to love. Her physical beauty emanated light. *This is like the light I experienced with Christ in the woods, but it's pale and duller and there is no love emanating from it.*

"You'll go to her like a moth to a flame. This is your future, you stupid fool. You will choose her." There was a certainty in the Demon Beast's declaration.

The vision of my future wife morphed into the experience of immense emotional pain that I would suffer as I attempted to be father to the son born of that marriage. The Demon Beast said, "You fool, your efforts to love, nurture, teach, and lead your son will all be undermined. Your son will be taken away to the furthest point on the earth, and you will be helpless. You'll fail with her, and you'll fail as a father."

Years of struggle were hurled at me in a heart-breaking fury. *No. I will love my son. I will not fail.*

"You have no choice, you fool, because you made your choice. This will all come to pass."

I lay in the tent in a half-awake dreamlike state defeated and crying. The grief associated with the failed marriage and my loss of the father role to my son was overwhelming and consuming. *I will love my son no matter what happens. I will overcome all of this. I will search for the love like the love that I experienced with Christ.*

Finally a reprieve came. In the next vision I was rescued from the pain of the first relationship, and the pain of losing my son, by an elegant, spiritually radiant woman. *She's beautiful. Her light is the same as Christ's. She's sharing peace and hope with me.* Her presence was a relief from the pain of the previous premonitions.

The Demon Beast's voice said, "Don't feel too good, you fool. You'll screw up this one too." A dull, green, light came from her presence and she left my life.

I was shown two huge towers in a city that I did not recognize. *Where is this? Why are you showing this to me?* The towers fell before my eyes and I saw the spirits of those killed flying to their Creator. *What does this have to do with me?*

Next, a flood of visions passed before me, showing me people of significance in my life, and the Demon Beast spoke again.

"There will be an injury."

Tearing chest pain. *What happened?*

"This injury will end your life's work. Everything you accomplish will be in vain. The injury will be a mask for your death."

What? What do you mean?

"You're such a fool. You can't change this, anyway."

I woke up out of the dreamlike state as searing pain hit my chest and my breath was suddenly taken from me. *No. I don't want to die.* I gasped for breath. *Would some one murder me? Stabbed? Shot? Heart attack? What was it?* I lay in the tent scared and alone. *Avoid all of this future.*

"This is your future. You have no choice." The demon beast mocked me for the last time.

Just before four in the morning a light sprinkle of dew hit my tent and dripped in on my face. I was wearing a pair of undershorts, backwards. Confused, I pulled them off to notice they were wet and stained with blood.

I slowly crawled out of my tent. My legs felt unusually stiff and weak. Draping my towel around my waist, I tried to stand, but could not bear my own weight. Leaning on the trunk of the nearest tree, I slowly stood again. As I stood a thick greasy wetness fell from my anus. My legs shook uncontrollably.

Come on, Pat, stand. Get your legs going. I took a couple of steps and was overcome by nausea. *Just get to the bathroom.* After a couple more steps I was aware of rectal pain and swelling. Severe lower bowel cramps hit me as I arrived at the camp bathroom. Nausea gave way to dry heaves at the sink. *Bowel cramps. Quick, get to the toilet. Don't crap yourself. I made it.* I sat, doubled over, and a flood of foul diarrhea filled the toilet. Pain and foggy memories of the night's terror triggered more uncontrollable shaking in my legs. I sat in fear. My rectum prolapsed and touched the toilet water. I reached back and pushed it back in, and continued to sit, shaking and crying.

Diarrhea seems done. Nausea's gone. Trying to stand, I felt my legs gave out. *Got to get off this toilet. Calm yourself, Pat. You're alive. Deep breaths. Okay, less shaking. Try to stand.* I stood, leaning on the wall of the toilet stall. *Now, get to the shower.*

The stained, damp undershorts were still in my hand. On the way to the shower I dropped them in the trash bin. Once I was under the shower spout, the temperature of the water was irrelevant. I reached to clean my backside with soap and found a donut-like pillow of sensitive tissue that burned to the touch. My rectum prolapsed again, and despite severe pain I pushed the swollen tissue back into my rectum. I writhed in pain and my legs shook uncontrollably.

Eventually, the shower water seemed to ease my rectal pain and brought strength back to my legs. *I'm alive. I survived.*

Footsteps crunched the ground outside the bathroom. *Oh please, no, I don't want to be hurt again. I can't take any more.*

"Hey, Pat, you in there?" Thank God. It was Roy's voice.

"Yeah, Roy. Just finishing up a shower."

"I didn't see you at the tent. Marie said, 'check the bath house.' You okay?"

Why did he ask me if I'm all right? My heart pounded hard and fast with paranoia.

"Be out in a couple of minutes." I turned the shower off, my legs, although still stiff, were now fully under me.

I packed up my tent and walked my bicycle to the RV dumping station, where Roy and Marie were preparing to leave. Roy helped me to load my bicycle into their huge thirty-six-foot new trailer home. Roy and I rode in the pickup truck pulling the trailer. Marie followed us in her Volkswagen.

My head buzzed from the terror of the previous night. *I was drugged and raped in the night. Who did this to me? The Demon Beast, the visions. My tent is undisturbed.* By demons, by men, or both, the crux of the event was the same. Against my will, I had been raped by pure evil. I had no memory of The Priest or The Minister.

"You're pretty quiet this morning. You sure you're okay?"

"I'm okay, Roy. I had a rough night last night."

"We've all had them. You'll be all right."

Why does he think I'll be all right? Did he drug and rape me? Should I be afraid of Roy? Does he know something? Come on Pat, ask him something.

"Yeah, I know. How was your night?"

"Slept like a baby."

Make more conversation. This doesn't feel right. Need to get away from him. Can't. We're driving down a road. My bike, everything I own, is in his RV. Don't tell him anything. Change the subject.

"You've got a nice truck here, Roy."

"Yep. Ya know, I spent twenty-one years working as an electrician at the U.S. Naval Shipyard in Virginia Beach. This truck and the trailer I'm pullin' are the fruits of my labor. We sold our home and plan to retire and travel the open roads."

Roy's desire to travel resonated with my tour. "Sounds like a great way to retire."

"My wife is a bit less enthusiastic, but the old girl will get used to it." He had a distinct patronizing air when he referred to his wife.

He drove the truck and trailer to the local RV shop where it was due for some servicing. *Thank God. He was telling the truth about stopping at a shop for the RV.* The shop, near Highway 64 and Highway 58, was within walking distance of Shoney's Restaurant, which served an all-you-can-eat breakfast buffet.

"Let's get a good breakfast in us before you ride off on that bike of yours."

Okay. Breakfast. Maybe food will make me feel better. Then I'll get my bike and leave.

Marie and Roy sat across from me in our booth by the window. I slowly lowered my body onto the padded bench seat. The ring of sore, swollen tissue that was my rectum squished and compressed into searing pain I tried to hide from them. I wanted to shift away from the pain but knew the slightest movement would spike the pain more. I leaned forward on the table to allow my elbows instead of my buttocks to bear my body weight.

"Are you okay, Pat?"

"I'm fine. Just a bit sore from riding." Marie nodded.

I sat in the restaurant booth alone with Marie while Roy made his way to the buffet. Sitting across from her, I could sense sadness in this pretty woman. I tried to make idle conversation. "Roy told me of your travel plans during retirement."

"I'm not so happy about it." Her eyes batted and misted.

"Why? It sounds like a great way to retire to me."

She picked up on the enthusiasm for the open road embodying my journey and my empathy for Roy's desire. "Pat, you're just starting out in life. You wouldn't understand."

"Try me, Marie." I was wondering what could possibly be more pleasant as a retirement than traveling in a big well-appointed trailer home.

"He sold our home out from under me. This travel thing is his idea, not mine. I raised a family in that home. There's twenty-one years of memories that are all gone. I miss my home so much. I can hardly stand being around him. He hurt me so bad."

A single tear spilled from her eye. She brushed it away, delicately, with a napkin. "After all of the years of sacrifice for that man, raising his children, meals on the table every day, I worked so hard." She paused. "I'm sorry, Pat. You don't need to hear this." Her chest rose slowly and fell as she sighed.

"I asked you to share, Marie. Now I understand." She enjoyed twenty-one years of building a life in that home. I visualized a quaint, Victorian, well-cared-for and well-lived-in home.

I recalled what it was like for me to move from Minnesota to Ohio at the age of ten and then again from Ohio to Ontario at the age of sixteen. The pain of leaving a home, friends, and community was real, and I had experienced it. Those moves, prompted by Dad's corporate climb, had been painful. Those moves had also helped to define and shape me as an individual. Pining for the loss of friends, school, and community had given me, over time, a toughness that served well in the face of adversity and change. Now I gathered all of that steely reserve to deal with the aftermath of the rape, but it wasn't enough.

The gulf between Roy and Marie was distinct and defined now. Roy returned to the table. They shared a quick glance with each another. I read their glances and knew it was time for me to allow them to share a few minutes alone.

"I'm ready for another trip to the buffet. Excuse me."

Roy nodded, and Marie smiled.

I lingered at the buffet to give them time alone. A waitress arrived with the bill at the same time I returned with another plate of hot food. I reached for the bill.

"Oh, no you don't, Pat."

"Ah, come on. You two have helped me enough, it's the least I can do."

"Pat, we insist. You're young, and we've enjoyed your company." Roy took the bill from my hand.

I asked Roy and Marie to stand outside of their trailer home while I took a photograph. Roy helped me unload my bike. I mounted and pedaled down Virginia Beach Boulevard thinking of them. I looked back over my shoulder several times, fearing I was being followed. *Nothing. Keep pedaling away from here. Never tell anyone, so they don't come back for you.*

My quads burned as I tried to slowly lower my buttocks onto the saddle. Instantly the pain had me standing and pedaling. I settled into a rhythm of stand-up pedaling and coasting. Occasionally I tried to sit back on the saddle, testing the traumatized rectal tissue. Memories of the night's terror leapt to my mind. *Think of something else.*

Marie had been betrayed by her husband. The hurt was raw and deep. I had wanted to say the right words to help her, but I was at a loss. A prayer of hope that they would reconcile their differences to enjoy their new life was all I could muster. With or without Roy, Marie would heal and adjust to a new life.

No. It couldn't have been Roy violating me last night.

Keep going, Pat. Look back again. Make sure you're alone. Never tell anyone. No police. Just get away from here. Pretend it never happened.

But it did happen. How could someone be so cruel? Why did this happen?

I coasted to a full stop and stood straddling the bike, shaking and sobbing.

Deep anger filled my heart. *Ride back to the campground and find who did this. Kill them, or at least fight to the death.* My hands hurt as I gripped the bike's bars with seething hatred for the rapists. *Who will I blame? Who will I kill? Thou shalt not kill. Fuck that, I want to kill whoever did this to me, and I don't care what God thinks.*

There was an inner strength in knowing I had survived. They had hurt my body and my soul, yet there was a part of me they couldn't touch. I had pled for my life, and they had let me live. I pedaled away again, pedaling standing, coasting, until my thighs burned so badly I thought I would collapse in a heap at the roadside.

Again, I coasted the bike to a stop.

Keep riding, Pat, one block at a time. Riding always makes you feel better. Ride and decide what to do.

I passed a police car parked on the other side of the road. *Go to the police. Who can I trust? Would the police believe me? I don't even know who did this to me. I don't want to be examined by the police.* I pictured myself in a room of the police station answering questions as someone parted my butt cheeks to examine my rectum. The thought of having my body judged or belittled by anyone else made me continue pedaling. *If you go to the police, your trip will be over. Don't stop. Keep pedaling.*

My eyes stung with ready tears. *Don't cry. It won't change a thing.* Tears flowed anyway, until I could no longer see the side of the road. I stopped to wipe my eyes on my T-shirt sleeve. *Don't let this end your trip. Keep going.*

I considered calling home and telling Dad what had happened. *You'll only make him worry. Don't call. You'll only start to cry.* Mom and Dad would worry about not hearing from me for a couple of days, but not as much as if I told them what had happened. *If I call Dad, he'll want to come down here and want me to go to the cops.*

I rationalized that being rescued by my parents or the police would be a failure to honor my goal of cycling all of the way to Florida. *You started this trip, so finish the trip.* I pedaled past a blur of strip malls and specialty shops along the highway. *Pretend it never happened. Just keep going.*

When the memory of the two men who had sodomized me flooded into my mind, I stopped the bike. *The Priest and The Minister did this to me!* I recalled coming to in my drugged stupor, identifying the voice of the priest, and confronting him. *How could they have done this? They're supposed to be good and Godly men? This doesn't make any sense to me.* I gritted my teeth until my jaw muscles ached. Tears streamed, as I shook my head side to side in denial. *Forget about them. Forget about what they did to you.* My throat muscles tightened. My chest heaved.

I repressed the memory and refused to believe the priest was involved. I was thankful just to be alive. *Just keep on cycling.*

I was only able to ride a short distance when I stopped and gripped the handlebars in anger. My anger was toward Jesus. *What kind of a Savior are you, anyway, to have let this happen?* I was alone in my anger. I had forgotten Jesus had told me something bad would happen. I had forgotten Jesus explained the nature of this fallen world. I had forgotten about His infinite unconditional love for me. *I'll handle this on my own. I don't need you.*

Eventually, toward the end of the day's pedaling, I was able to sit down on the saddle. Pain, changed from ache to burn to searing, causing me to shift my position on the saddle innumerable times. *Look back again. Good. No one seems to be following. Get away from here, Pat. Never tell anyone.*

IX
Flight of the Bike

⁵ Fearfullness and trembling have come upon me, and horror has overwhelmed me.

⁶ So I said, "Oh that I had wings like a dove! I would fly away, and be at rest.

⁷ Indeeed, I would wander far off, and remain in the wilderness. Selah.

⁸ I would hasten my escape from the windy storm and tempest.

⁹ Destroy, O Lord, and divide their tongues: for I have seen violence and strife in the city.

Psalm 55:5-9 NKJV

At the end of Highway 58 was Highway 60. *Keep going, Pat. They might be following.* After cruising the strip along the beach, I came to a bike path. The path and Highway 60 eventually took me to Seashore State Park. Another highway took me into Fort Story, where I stopped at Cape Henry. *Stop and rest. Learn some history. Get your mind off the terror.*

In 1607 the first English colonists landed here before heading north to colonize at Jamestown. Cape Henry was an important landmark during the Revolutionary War. The French

who allied with the American Revolutionaries successfully defeated the English in a sea battle that has since been dubbed
"The Battle of the Capes." The Cape Henry Lighthouse, built in
1791, was the first lighthouse in the U.S.A. I read all of the historical markers, but my head buzzed with confusion.

While visiting the lighthouse I was approached by two
young men dressed in U.S. military uniforms. *They seem safe
to talk to. We're in the middle of a public place. Okay, talk to
them.* They asked about my bike tour as we walked into the
information center. The younger of the two laid fifty cents on
the counter as I was buying some postcards. He handed me a
sticker from the lighthouse.

"This is for your bike."

"Really? Thanks, but you don't have to do that."

"I have a lot of admiration for the way you are traveling."

"Where are you guys from?" I felt safe talking to them.

"We're stationed up at Fort Story. This is the last day of our
leave."

I thanked them again and wanted to visit longer, but they
were due back at base and had to leave. *What will happen in the
military lives of these young guys? Will they ever see battle?
The rights and freedoms of America are founded on the shed
blood of thousands of young guys just like these two. They're
only about nineteen years old. Most young guys are just into
themselves. Not these guys. They recognized me as a sole traveler and then befriended me with a simple gesture. Yeah, that's
it, Pat. Think about them and not about what happened.*

An encroaching sea was slowly consuming the beach that
fronted the Cape Henry Lighthouse. The locals were mounting
an effort to move the lighthouse, thereby preserving another of
America's firsts.

Cycling away from Fort Story and the lighthouse, I contemplated change in life. *Move the lighthouse inland; the sea will
continue to consume the land. How much control do I have in
this life? What sea of change will I be confronted with? What*

will I do to persevere? Maybe the Demon Beast is right. I saw my future and there's no changing it.

I left Cape Henry behind as I headed back down the strip. Highway 60 was now called General Booth Boulevard. Highway 615, Princess Ann Boulevard, brought me to Seneca Campground close to the North Carolina border.

As I peeled off my bicycle shorts, I noticed streaks of blood in the chamois. Standing in the shower, I scrubbed the shorts until the blood disappeared. I fought back tears that again wanted to pour from my eyes. *It didn't happen. It didn't happen.*

Curled in my sleeping bag, exhausted, I feared the night. *Stay awake. Don't let the Demon Beast come back. Please, no. Please leave me alone.* The little sleep I had was interrupted by vivid memories of the night before.

It was very early and dark when I packed up and left Seneca Campground. I rode down Highway 615 into North Carolina through some swampy land. Bugs flew at my face. Ducking and squinting along the dark road, I pedaled on. The road brought me to Knott's Island, where I boarded a ferry for a forty-five-minute ride to Currituck, North Carolina.

I need to rest. Try not to fall asleep. Just rest. I'll leave another state with the next day's cycling.

I pedaled past lush greenery beside a generous bicycle lane along Highway 58. A long bridge from Port Harbor to Kitty Hawk heralded my entrance to North Carolina's Outer Banks. *Don't stop until you reach the Wright Brother's Monument and Museum in Kill Devil Hills.* My legs responded, but my head and heart ached with fatigue from the night with my violators and the Demon Beast. *Keep going. Get your mind off everything but the museum. Remember, keep learning.*

The Wright Brothers had once repaired bicycles and had used bicycle parts in their first motor-powered airplane. *Now that's cool. Yeah, riding a bike is kinda like flying, especially down hill.* Glancing out the window, I made sure my bike and gear were untouched.

My bike is special. It's my meditation, my means of discovery and means of escape. Orville and Wilbur's bicycle shop in Dayton, Ohio had helped to finance their experimentation with flight at Kitty Hawk. The two men approached human flight with scientific rigor. *These guys were smart. Wow! They had even constructed a wind tunnel to experiment with different wing shapes.*

Nag's Head was very touristy and I tossed the term *hyper-commercialized* around in my head as if I was writing a travel guide. I rode through without a stop. Highway 158 became Highway 12, and I entered the Hatteras National Seashore. From Whalebone to Rodanthe, a stretch of about twenty-four miles, the Outer Banks were virtually unspoiled. Sand, lots of sand, grass, and low shrubs retained the delicate land.

I was alone, and with the rhythm of my pedaling I was feeling safe. A strong crosswind slapped past me, making it tough to breathe. *The Demon Beast took your breath away. Breathe deep. Again, breathe deep.* My chest heaved. *Don't let a crosswind rob you of your life's breath. Keep going. Forget about the terror. Just keep going.*

Near the midway point of the long bridge traversing the Oregon Inlet, a slow steady hiss came from one of my bike tires. The leak was slow enough to allow me to coast almost all of the way across the bridge, but I could feel the telltale squish and wobble from the rear tire. I carefully brought the bike to a halt. Continuing would have meant damaging the rim and tire wall. There was little traffic as I walked the bike off the bridge. *Find a safe place to make the repair.*

The new wheel I had obtained at Duffy's Bicycle Shop in Avis, Pennsylvania, did not have a quick-release mechanism. A pang of regret struck me as I loosened the bolts of the back wheel. *Why'd I give up the entire wheel because of a broken axle?* The lack of a quick-release mechanism made the repair of the flat more laborious. The sun was hot. The box of used axles and quick releases at Duffy's Bicycle Shop that Brenda had handed me flashed to mind. *With that used axle you could have kept the strong alloy wheel. Nothing wrong with used, Pat. Not everything has to be new.* Methodically I removed the wheel.

With the wheel off, I removed the inner tube. I attached the pump to the valve of the tube and inflated the tube until I could locate the offending hole. It was a small hole, and the tube was certainly worthy of a patch. I roughened the rubber around the hole, squeezed the contact cement onto the tube, and placed the patch.

The wheel I had purchased at Duffy's was a good one, albeit unnecessary. *That's your black and white way of thinking that leads to redundant choices and increased costs. Don't forget this lesson.* I carefully inspected the inside of the tire to locate what might have caused the puncture. I sat rotating the tire as I rubbed the fleshy pad of skin on my left hand across the inside tire wall. There it was, sharp and still poking, the offending razor-sharp thorn. I pulled out the thorn, and the tire was ready.

I carefully deflated and folded the tube tightly to ensure the patch could seal. I semi-inflated a new tube and placed it inside the tire, which was halfway on the rim. I inserted the valve through the stem hole of the wheel, and seated the tire back onto the rim. Then I placed the wheel back on the frame stays, aligned and secured with the two nuts of the axle, *instead of a quick release mechanism.* The entire job took one hour. The deep concentration I poured into the tire change helped push the terror out of my mind, at least temporarily.

After a filling spaghetti dinner at a little restaurant in Rodanthe, North Carolina, I pitched my tent at the North Beach Campground, showered, and then took the short walk over the dune to the beach, where the sunset was fading fast. Stars became more and more visible as the last of the day's light faded into the west. To the east, I studied the blue-black hues of the horizon and the sky out over an inky Atlantic Ocean. A falling star coursed through the sky with a tail burning bright.

Childhood custom told me to make a wish, but no wish came to mind. I walked back to my tent still listening to the waves. *Why can't you make a wish? I'm content. That's why. You faced the Demon Beast. I survived the violation. I walked away. I'm alive. Pure contentment.* I fell asleep to the sound of the waves breaking on the beach.

I woke up before dawn the next morning. *Finally, that was a peaceful night's sleep.* I packed my tent and belongings in the still dark morning. The sound of small waves came rhythmically from the sandy beach. I locked the bike to the picnic table and walked to the beach. Sitting in the soft sand, I saw the sky on the ocean's horizon begin to lighten. The beach was peaceful. The ocean was calm.

From Rodanthe, North Carolina, I cycled to Hatteras, North Carolina, where I boarded the ferry to Ocracoke Island. I rode the twelve-mile length of the island and met two other touring cyclists, Robert and Nancy from Vermont. They travelled by car, parked and then cycled in an area. On this day, for instance, they rode the twenty-four miles up and down the length of the island.

They were a middle-aged couple. Robert was an engineering professor and consulted for many private companies. I never did learn why Robert had only one leg, but I was amazed at the pace he kept as he pedaled from one side of his bike.

When I arrived at the town of Ocracoke, I purchased the ticket for my next ferry and then went to a little restaurant for a thirst-quenching iced tea, and a cooling, filling ice cream. Robert and Nancy had arrived ahead of me. We sat on the restaurant patio, and they told me of some of their cycling adventures through Ireland. I listened intently and then said, "Ireland is one of the places in the world I would love to bike tour through." I noticed feeling an effort in speaking to people I had never experienced before.

At 3:00 p.m. the ferry from Ocracoke to Cedar Island began to load. The ferry ride was over two hours long. I met more people who were interested in my trip. One lady commented about my being from Canada and taking such a daring trip. "What is it about you Canadians and these long, hard trips? You remind me of Terry Fox."

"Well, ah, thanks, but Terry Fox is too special a person for me to be compared to." I was embarrassed by the comparison. "Actually, I'm an American. I was born in St. Paul, Minnesota, and have lived in Canada only since 1978."

"Oh," she exclaimed with a deflated look. I realized that for most Americans, Canada was a faraway place. Many Americans made an assumption of my foreignness when they learned I was from Canada, a mysterious cold land to the north. She walked away, and I was glad to be alone again and not have to make superficial conversation.

Driftwood Campground was conveniently located next to the dock where the ferry landed. The salt air, cycling, repressing the terror, and socializing with new acquaintances had tired me, and I was relieved not have to face the wind on the bicycle.

I was pedaling again early on the morning of October second. The ride was good until I had another flat as I was passing through Morehead City, North Carolina. This time the front-wheel flat was relatively easy to fix. Once again the methodical tire change kept my mind from returning to the terror.

I attributed a harder than normal pedaling effort to fatigue in my legs, but unfortunately the sensation was due to my rear wheel being slightly deflated. I rode over railroad tracks and felt the hard metal transmit a jolt from the rear wheel through the entire frame of my bike. The impact caused the rear wheel rim to bend. The bike slowed as the bend in the rim met hard friction across the brake pads.

I examined the wheel and laid blame for the bent rim on myself for not having checked the tire pressure. The quick remedy was for me to loosen the tension of the rear brake calipers, thereby allowing the bend in the rim to pass the brake pads friction-free. Mounting the bike again, I experimented with the brakes, making sure I could still bring the bike to a quick halt if necessary. After studying the map, I decided to push on into Jacksonville, North Carolina, to have the wheel repaired.

The day was also marked by scorching heat. I could feel my sweat dry from the air being pushed across my skin as I rode. When I stopped, the heat in the air and the heat radiating up from the road again reminded me of a sauna. I was in a constant state of thirst, and pushed liquids into my body all day long.

The heat and repairs took a toll on me, and after setting up my tent under a big willow tree at Tommy's Campground in Swansboro, North Carolina, I took a three-hour nap. Even as I napped, I continued to sweat. Screaming U.S. fighter jets woke me. The airbases at Bogue and Camp Lejeune were both near.

The next morning I left at the earliest light and rode the approximate fourteen miles to Jacksonville, North Carolina. Despite taking a wrong turn in the city, I located a shop called Bike Arcade. I arrived before the shop opened, which allowed me to have a good breakfast at a motel restaurant a block away.

Mr. George V. Thurmond was the owner of the Bike Arcade. *Does my face portray the pain and terror I'm trying to quash?* He exhibited a kind and helpful way making me feel safe in his company. He tore down a good wheel and rebuilt it with some extra strong spokes. He then lubed my chain and adjusted my rear brakes. The work on the bike took almost two hours. I felt deep gratitude when he only charged me thirty-one dollars, the price of the new wheel. I was back on the road by noon.

The bike felt new again and, despite another incredibly hot day, I made good time into Wilmington, North Carolina. I considered touring the battleship U.S.S. North Carolina, but only took the time to ride past the big impressive vessel. A further sixteen-mile ride brought me into Carolina Beach within minutes of the sun setting. The KOA campground I pedaled into was complete with camp store and laundry, both of which were needed. The friendly lady at the store informed me that Myrtle Beach was eighty miles away. It was my goal for the next day's ride.

A retired bar owner, his brother, and their wives invited me to their campsite for a beer. *They seem genuinely friendly. You can trust them, but don't get too close.* The cold frothy drink tasted amazingly good as it passed tingling over my parched tongue. The foursome was also going to Florida, traveling in a big RV. The little bit of alcohol in that cold beer numbed my tired body. After answering their questions about my trip and thanking them for the soothing beer, I retreated to my tent and was almost asleep before my eyes closed.

On October fourth, I cycled from Carolina Beach, North Carolina to Myrtle Beach, South Carolina. This was the third day of sweltering, dehydrating heat. By late morning, I had pulled into the parking lot of a 7-11 variety store. I leaned my bike up against the storefront, walked in and bought a quart of milk.

I stood outside guzzling it, when an old, green, Ford pickup truck pulled up. I knew I was being watched. Four thickly-muscled black men piled out of the truck and headed toward me. Sweat was beaded about their foreheads and arms. My heart began to pound. No one else was in sight. One of the men walked into the store. Three of them walked to within a foot of where I stood.

Wide eyed, I looked up nervously. *Please no trouble. Please. I just want to keep riding.* My sheltered childhood had not prepared me for a confrontation with blacks. In the casual conversations between relatives and family friends I had heard growing up, blacks were referred to as *different*, and *to be avoided.* Black people lived apart from the world I knew.

"Where you from?" Questioned the most muscular of the black men.

"Canada." The three were dressed in tar-stained coveralls and well-worn work boots.

"You didn't ride this thing from Canada?"

"Yeah, I did."

"When did you leave?"

"September eighth."

"How far do you ride a day?"

"In the Allegany Mountains I was down to about fifty miles a day, but on the flat stretches I ride seventy to one-hundred miles a day. Mostly seventy or eighty."

"Seventy or eighty! That's crazy. I once rode a bike ten miles to visit my cousins and I thought I was gonna die."

Okay. Maybe these guys aren't a threat.

"What do have in here?" The third of the three asked pointing to my full panniers.

"Clothing, a couple of books, and my camping gear."

The most heavily muscled of the three shook his head, "I couldn't ever do something like this. Shoot, all the way from Canada. Amazing."

I felt my body relax as they all beamed warm smiles at me. The fourth black man came out from the 7-11 saying, "Hey, what you guys doing out here? I thought you was all thirsty."

"Come here. This guy rode his bike all of the way from Canada."

I saw a large Cadillac pull into the parking lot of the 7-11. A tall, overweight, middle-aged white man with a cowboy hat stepped out of the car. He glanced at me as I was surrounded by the curious black men and then walked toward us.

"These niggers aren't bothering you, are they?" His voice was deep and condescending. His belly hung over a huge belt buckle that hid his feet from his own view.

"No sir. We ain't bothering him."

"Shut your face, nigger. I wasn't talkin' to you." The white man looked at me, "Well?"

"They're just asking about my trip."

"What trip?" Again condescension oozed. He stood in pompous anger waiting for my reply.

"I rode my bike from Canada. I'm on my way to Florida."

"Stupid, dumb, fucking cracker. You're on your own." The white man turned away and walked into the store.

I stood dumbfounded.

"Don't worry about him." One of the black men laid his hand on my shoulder. "Tell us more 'bout your trip."

We talked and laughed together after the fat, white bigot left. After firm handshakes and thanks for their wishes for a safe trip, I mounted my bike and rode on. The black men disappeared into the store to quench their thirst.

About a mile later, as I pedaled along, I heard the green pickup truck honk behind me. The four black men each had a hand out a window waving enthusiastically as they passed. I held the handle bar with my left hand and waved back. They honked once more, and then sped off to their next worksite. I was again alone on my bike.

Black people are nothing like I was told. That fat white bigot in the big Caddy was a revelation that profoundly impacted me. *This world is not a fair place. All men might be created equal, but not all men are treated equal.* I pedaled on into the heat.

Again I pushed fluids into me. George, the bike-shop owner back in Jacksonville, had given me a new water bottle that came in handy. By the end of the day's ride I had drunk six bottles of water, one gallon of milk, one quart of orange juice, a half-quart of apple juice, and two cans of soda. I was still thirsty. The ride was long, and against a stiff, hot wind.

A kind woman at a small store just past the South Carolina border invited me to sit in a comfortable old chair to rest and recuperate in the air conditioning. She enjoyed listening to the highlights of the tour and graciously filled my water bottles during our conversation.

"How much further is Myrtle Beach?" I asked. I was hoping I would only have five or ten miles to go.

"Oh, you have another, oh, about twenty-two miles or so." Her southern drawl was distinct. "That's a ways to go 'n this heat. I'm sure glad it's you 'n' not me."

I smiled. "That's a bit farther than I thought."

"Can you make it?"

"I can make it, but I have to hit the road before I run out of time. Nice meeting you. Thanks for your help."

"Never mind that, young man. You just be careful out there." We parted with a soft handshake.

Those last twenty-two miles were tough. The respite in the air-conditioned store made the heat feel worse as I pedaled onto the highway. Fatigue ripped through my body. *Keep going, Pat, don't stop!*

The Myrtle Beach area seemed to be one long strip of hotels, motels, apartments, and tourist-trap shops. I was almost out of the tourist strip area when the fatigue and heat became unbearable. *Take a break, and then go a little further.* A triple peach ice cream and a tall glass of ice water re-energized me enough to ride on to Myrtle Beach State Park, three miles farther south.

The park was on the oceanfront and had access to a soft, sandy beach. I set up the tent, and a long cool shower helped me to recover from the day's ride. At the camp bathhouse I thoroughly cleaned the chamois of my cycling shorts. The trauma from the rape coupled with the extreme heat and sweat had caused the skin over my sit bones to become chafed.

Infection from the raw skin due to chafing was a real concern for long distance cyclists, so infection from the rape should have been a major concern for me, but due to my efforts to repress it all, I never dealt with such a fear. After a good lathering of soap in the shower, I wore loose shorts without underwear. The dry air and lack of contact with chamois and bicycle seat felt good.

The sun had just finished setting as I went for a walk on the beach. The white, soft sand pushed between my toes and massaged the arches of my feet. Warm water caressed my feet and lower legs as I waded into the ocean.

I walked onto the fishing pier and watched people fish, as the daylight began to fade. The wind blew just enough to take the discomfort away from the heat. *It's very peaceful here.* I could feel the pier gently sway with the ocean swells. Closing my eyes, I concentrated on the rocking sensation. *Kind of like being slowly rocked in a cradle. Kinda like flying. Kinda like biking.*

X

Catholic Conundrums

5 But all their works they do to be seen of men. They make their phylacteries broad, and enlarge the borders of their garments, 6 They love the best places at feasts, the best seats in the synagogues, 7 greetings in the markets, and to be called by men, Rabbi, Rabbi; 8 But you do not be called Rabbi; for one is your Teacher, the Christ, and you all are brethren. 9 Do not call anyone on earth your father; for One is your Father, He who is in heaven. 10 And do not be called teachers; for One is your Teacher, the Christ.
Matthew 23:6-10 NKJV

In the early morning of Sunday October five, I started south along Highway 17 toward Charleston, South Carolina. I was perhaps one-hundred-feet down the road when I saw a small sign in the highway dividing area. "St. Michael's Roman Catholic Church five miles ahead."

The good Catholic boy squirmed. *Was this some coincidence? Is God leading me to the church? If I can force myself to go to a Catholic church after what they did to me, then I can face anything else life throws my way. I can prove to myself that I can go to a Catholic Church despite what happened. If I can do this, then I can forget about what they did to me. If the timing's right, I'll go to Mass, coincidence or not. Maybe I'll learn something. God's got me in a church this Sunday.*

As I approached the locale, my empty stomach reminded me that it was time to eat. Conveniently, there was a Shoney's Restaurant close to the church.

Father Joseph greeted me outside of the church. He asked a few questions about my trip and then ushered me in. Father Joseph struck me as being a nice man, but with an anxious disposition that made me wonder if he was slightly neurotic. Any thoughts of neurosis, however, were dispelled as he began the Mass and delivered a Gospel and message that spoke to me. The Gospel, based upon Luke 17:6-10, spoke of faith the size of a mustard seed being able to cast a huge mulberry tree into the raging sea. *Do I have any faith?*

Looking up from my thoughts, I noticed a young man one pew ahead of me holding an infant. The infant's head was nestled in his Dad's chest. *That's it; that's what I want.* The vision of my future son was still fresh. *I will have a son.* Staring at the young father, I longed for the time in my life when I too could hold my boy lovingly in my arms as his head rested sleepily on my chest. My throat tightened, as I recalled my emotional pain as my son moved far away from me in the vision.

At the Mass at St. Michael's an infant was Baptized. As was customary, Father Joseph invited the congregation to renew their baptismal vows. "My brothers and sisters in Christ, simply respond 'I do' to each of the Baptismal promises."

"Do you reject Satan?"

"I do." I wholeheartedly joined the congregation's response as I recalled the Demon Beast.

"And all of his works?"

"I do." Another easy one after being raped.

"And all his empty promises?"

"I do." I wondered if that included those visions?

"Do you believe in God, the Father Almighty, creator of Heaven and earth?"

"I do."

"Do you believe in Jesus Christ, his only Son, our Lord, who was born of the Virgin Mary, was crucified, died, and was buried, rose from the dead, and is now seated at the right hand of the Father?"

I stood in silence as the rest of the congregation responded, "I do."

"Do you believe in the Holy Spirit?"

Don't know.

"The Holy Catholic Church?"

Definitely not. You don't own and control my spirituality. You fucking assholes raped me. I hope you all rot in hell.

"The communion of saints?"

Not sure. What's the big deal anyway?

"The forgiveness of sins?"

Guess so; hope so, but what about what they did?

"The resurrection of the body?"

Maybe.

"And life everlasting."

Maybe.

Some people had said a genuine heartfelt "I do." Others had seemed to droan out their responses in a monotone.

Father Joseph said, "God, the all-powerful Father of our Lord Jesus Christ, has given us a new birth by water and the Holy Spirit, and forgiven all of our sins. May He also keep us faithful to our Lord Jesus Christ for ever and ever."

The congregation said "Amen." I stood in silence.

Do all of these people around me know what they're saying? Do they really believe in what they are proclaiming, or are they just going along because this religion stuff might mean something, but they're not quite convinced? Why am I at this Mass, anyway? I had made my choice. Now I was squirming with it.

Back on the bicycle, riding away, I realized I felt good about attending the Mass. I set forth at a fast pace. The traffic was light, and there were few trucks because it was Sunday. Eventually the heat began to slow down my progress. The time spent at church, coupled with the heat, led me to the conclusion that Charleston was a destination out of the day's reach.

I passed what looked like the beginnings of a forest fire about two miles north of McClellanville. The fire was on the east side of the highway. The wind blowing from the southwest kept the blaze contained between the highway, the intercostal waterway, and the Santee River. The smoke was thick and the flames were bright. The southwest wind protected me from the smoke and heat. I only detected a slight smell of burning wood and brush as I cycled past, but as I arrived in McClellanville, I passed fire trucks speeding northbound, with lights flashing and sirens singing.

The day ended at Buck Hall of the Frances Marion National Forest, a rustic campground on the bank of the inter-coastal waterway. The showers were outdoors. The campground was quiet. *Is anyone around watching me shower? It seems safe.* I looked up at tall trees and blue skies as the cool water coursed down my naked body, refreshing me. I stood looking up at the sky as billowy clouds passed by. *Surely God had a hand in guiding me today. If that was you, God, thank you.*

I woke on the morning of October six, noting it had cooled down a bit overnight. Leaving Awendaw, South Carolina, I rode to the outskirts of Charleston where I ate a big buffet breakfast at another Shoney's restaurant.

After breakfast I made my way to Patriot's Point and toured the aircraft carrier *U.S.S. Yorktown*, the submarine *Clamagore*, and the destroyer *Laffey*. My bicycle was dwarfed by the huge aircraft carrier. It had a naval museum that could easily have justified a full day's attention.

I tested my ability to trust people by visiting with curious strangers who wanted to know about my trip. Asking a fellow tourist to take my camera and snap a photo of me standing next to a naval fighter jet was another leap of faith. I wanted to learn and remember the historic details of the vessels, but I could not concentrate. My head buzzed with the terror I was still repressing.

How many men had served on this carrier? How many men had walked on the deck of this ship only to lose their lives in service to their country? What kind of fear did they face before they met their Maker? My questions helped me, at least temporarily, to forget my pain, and they humbled me in the face of the freedoms I had, even when those freedoms were used by evil people.

Highway 17 had a lot of traffic. Crossing the bridges over the Cooper River, I entered Charleston. The lush sleepy southern trees of Charleston were inviting. My tongue's dance with the sweet and bitter of a *Hagan Daz* Coffee-Chip double-scoop ice-cream-cone was the perfect complement to Charleston's charm, and for a while I was able to forget.

As I sat outside the ice cream parlor, a retired couple came out of the store and questioned me about the tour. They owned a RV that carried their bicycles so they could tour from wherever they parked. *That's the kind of living and traveling I would like to do when I retire or become independently wealthy.* They took a picture of me with my camera in front of the ice cream parlor.

The husband insisted in taking another picture, but the film was obviously at the end of the roll. I watched helplessly as he forced the mechanical arm to advance the film. The resulting picture was an interesting double exposure of me standing with my bike and me sitting at the park bench in front of the ice cream shop.

I found Oak Plantation Campground and called home after setting up my tent. A sense of being alone increased my efforts to repress the terror. After miles and miles of internal dialogue with myself, I longed to interact with someone close to me. I needed help, but knew I had to deal with it all on my own, because I had told Jesus I was living my life without Him and on my own terms. Wrestling with a profound sense of loss, I fell asleep, looking forward to a fresh start the next day.

The air had cooled during the night, which made for a restful sleep. My warm sleeping bag made a cocoon I was reluctant to emerge from. Nonetheless, I started cycling at seven o'clock. The sky was overcast, and the wind was at my back for most of the day.

Riding felt good. There was no paved shoulder along Highway 17, and the traffic was heavy with huge tractor-trailers passing within inches of me. The wake of wind from the passing trucks pulled me along. I took Highway 17 to Highway 21, which brought me into Beaufort, South Carolina. In Beaufort I found a bicycle shop and purchased a new spare inner tube. The staff directed me to a campground along my route towards Savannah.

Kobuch's Campground was easy to find. I was greeted by Tom O'Brien Sr.'s firm handshake. He was father of the campground's owner. Tom, father of seven, was a retired U.S. Marine who had fought in the Pacific during World War II. He asked about my trip. I think he could tell I was on a personal quest for some answers in life. *Maybe this guy will impart some astonishing piece of wisdom to help me along.*

My tent was set up, and I was organizing my gear, when Tom showed up with an album of photos from his time in World War II and of his family. We talked about many things and then settled into conversation about religion.

"Tom, I'm having trouble with my beliefs right now, which is why I'm on this trip."

"Well, what religion were you raised in, Pat?"

"Roman Catholic."

"That's great, Pat. I'm Catholic too. I've been Catholic my whole life and never needed to question anything." His eyes sparkled at the common ground we shared in the Roman

Catholic Church, yet there was Marine Corps sternness in his last statement. "Ya know, Pat, young people today seem to question everything. My generation never did. I don't think it's a bad thing to question. No, it's not bad. But it can be dangerous."

"Yeah, but sometimes you have to question," I said.

"For me, the Marine Corp and my being Roman Catholic are much the same. In the Marines you have a commanding officer and you obey the orders of that commanding officer or you're in trouble. In the Roman Catholic Church the Pope is the commanding officer. What the Pope declares is what I obey as a good Christian soldier."

Tom searched my face for some response in agreement with his simple yet sincere analogy. My blank stare revealed the confusion deep within me. "Tom, my confusion about the Catholic Church is wrapped up in a relationship with someone. We almost got married. In fact, she became a Catholic for me." I pulled the picture of Gerda from my wallet. Tom grasped it in his aged hands.

"Pretty girl, Pat. How old are you?"

"Twenty-four," I replied, not sure how that related to my confused life.

"It seems to me that at twenty-four, you should be ready to get married. And you say she turned Catholic for you? Sounds perfect."

"Not so perfect when your heart is no longer in your church."

"I guess I don't understand you, Pat."

Our conversation seemed to grind to a halt.

Tom changed the subject, "Hey Pat, what are your favorite numbers."

"My favorite numbers, Tom? Why?"

"Oh whenever I get to know someone special, I ask them what their favorite numbers are so that I can play them in the South Carolina State Lottery."

I smiled at him. "How many numbers do you need?"

"Six."

"Okay, well let me think. Number six, because that's how many kids are in our family. Number sixteen, because that was my age when our family moved to Canada. Number twenty-four because that's my age now. Number one and number thirty-nine. Number one because I believe in one God. My Grandma Blanche would always tell people that she was 'thirty-nine and holding' whenever anyone asked her age. And number eight, because that's how many are in our family counting Mom and Dad."

He visited my campsite a few more times in the evening, just to visit and share another tidbit about his life and his family. "You know, my one son married a non-Catholic girl. I can't say I was pleased, but they seem to be making a go of it."

"Did she become a Catholic for him?" I asked.

"Nope. My son doesn't go to church much any more. I'm not blaming her, but I just don't understand what you kids are all thinking when you step away."

"I guess we're searching."

"That's what I don't get, Pat. For me the church has all the answers. What else is there to search for?"

"I can't speak for your son, Tom, but for me the church's answers just don't satisfy my questions. It's okay, man. I know my Mom and Dad don't understand either."

I wanted to change the subject now. Our conversation was clearly on the topic of my search, but reflected the same disconnect I had with my parents over the subject.

"Hey, Tom, how did the campground get this name?" The campsite was very inviting, clean, well kept.

"It's named after Tom Junior's dog, 'Kobuch.'"

"That's a different name. What kind of a dog is Kobuch?"

"A giant German Schnauzer."

"I didn't know German Schnauzers came in giant size."

We conversed about dogs for a while.

"Tom, I'm gonna send you a postcard when I get to Florida."

"Pat, you don't have to bother sending a postcard to an old guy like me. Just get on your way and sort out your life." Tom and I parted with a firm handshake.

I hardly noticed the miles of the early morning ride on October eight, because it was so relaxing. At the Georgia State line I read a sign, "Georgia: The State of Adventure." I wondered what was in store for me in this state.

I crossed a huge bridge to enter Savannah and then easily found the visitor's center. At the center, I watched a video presentation about the Great Exposition, and then I wandered through the museum. A second presentation, entitled, "The Siege of Savannah" gave detailed information about the American Colonists and their allies who banded together in an attempt to take Savannah from the British during the Revolutionary War. Britain withstood the efforts of the colonists, Poulaski and his cavalry, the Scottish Highlanders, and the French. The presentations and museum were full of interesting details I never recalled learning in my U.S. history classes. The videos distracted me from all I was repressing.

Downtown contained many parks with green trees dripping with Spanish moss. Events and people were honored with numerous monuments. Touring the historic district of Savannah, I found it hard to believe such a serene, romantic-looking place harbored the nation's highest per capita crime rate.

Joe greeted me as I wandered into a bicycle shop simply to inquire about campgrounds. Joe's buddy J.R. was a part owner of the bike shop. With true southern hospitality Joe, manager of Savannah's Chart House Restaurant, offered me a place to stay. I also had the honor of meeting two of Georgia's best bicycle racers, Carl who was ranked second at the time, and his friend, J.P. The two racers and I looked at one another with a mutual respect and admiration. *It feels like I can trust these guys. Try.* Based on their friendliness and my intuition, I accepted Joe's offer of accommodation.

St. Peter's, the oldest Catholic Church in Georgia, stood, ominous, as I set out for more sightseeing. I stared at the lifeless structure that held no attraction for me, and I headed toward the river.

River Street was lined with old buildings on one side and a park with brick paths, trees, a fountain, and more monuments on the water side. This was the perfect spot for me to enjoy an ice cream as I sat on a park bench overlooking the river.

At four o'clock, I stopped back at the bike shop and visited with Carl and J.P. until Joe and J.R. returned from their afternoon golf. Joe's place was a typical Spartan bachelor pad. After a shower, I wrote some postcards and watched baseball with J.R. and Joe. The beer they offered tasted great. My head began to swim from the effects of the alcohol.

"Hey, guys. This beer is going straight to my head."

"That's a good place for it to go," replied Joe, laughing.

"Man, Pat, you must have some pure blood from all of that cycling," said J.R. as he reached into his pocket and produced a small bag with a couple of joints and a lighter.

"That's what I need after a hard day of work," said Joe, who sat back in his easy chair and kicked off his shoes.

J.R. lit up the joint, inhaled the smoke deeply and then held his breath to achieve the maximum transfer of the cannabis' drug effect into his blood.

"Here, man," said J.R. as he passed the joint to Joe, whose attention was taken by the baseball game. Joe accepted the joint and took his own long drag. I saw Joe and J.R. grin at each other as Joe passed the joint toward me. J.R. added, "Hey Pat, can that pure blood of yours handle this stuff? It's the real thing man."

"Thanks, guys, but I'll pass. The beer's given me enough of a buzz." We all laughed.

"That's cool, man," said Joe, "but have you ever tried grass?"

"Oh yeah, I've tried it, but I truthfully I never really liked the buzz from it."

My mind wandered back to the first drag I ever had on a joint. I was in grade eleven at the Catholic high school in St. Thomas, Ontario. After the move from Chagrin Falls, Ohio to St. Thomas, I had struggled for acceptance by my new peers. I was the new kid. I was the American kid. Tony and Hans never asked me whether I had smoked grass before. They seemed to assume I had, as an American high school kid.

I had taken a long drag off that first joint in the alley behind the Camera Shop, which was off property but close to the school. I coughed and sputtered as the hot smoke burnt into my nasopharnyx and bronchi. "Sorry, guys, it's been a while." They looked on at the 'experienced' American kid. In truth I had never smoked pot. Peer pressure and the desire to fit in were powerful motivators for me as a new-to-a-school and new-to-a-country seventeen-year old kid.

The second time I smoked a joint was again with Tony and Hans. We smoked up in the same spot behind the camera shop. This time it was during the break just before Mr. Crasper's World Religions class. I sat in the class chewing Hubba Bubba grape bubble gum to cover up the burnt-grass smell of my breath, with my head feeling like it was floating into two separate halves.

"Pat! Get rid of your gum," demanded Crasper. He was in the middle of a diatribe about the differences between Protestant doctrine and Roman Catholic doctrine. Karen, one of the girls at St. Joe's who I had a crush on, sat in the seat behind me. As we had walked into class I let her know I had a good buzz on to help me cope with the drivel from Crasper. Karen repeatedly tapped me on the shoulder when Crasper faced the chalkboard. When I turned she sat there smiling and made a wavy motion with her fingers as she said, "Pat, you're bumming out, you're bumming way, way, out, man."

By the third time she teased me, Crasper had turned and looked quizzically our way. "Pat, Karen, is there something the two of you would like to share with the class?"

"No, sir," Karen quickly answered.

Tony and Hans looked panicked as Crasper walked towards our row of desks. "Are you feeling okay, Mr. Milroy?" No doubt my glassy eyes were betraying my attempt to not look stoned.

"Yeah, I'm fine."

"Okay, Mr. Milroy. Perhaps you can tell me the difference between the Eucharist as celebrated by Catholics and the Eucharist as celebrated by Protestants. No, better yet, Mr. Milroy, you are a Catholic like the rest of us. Please share with us your views about the Roman Catholic Eucharist."

"Well, I kinda consider the Eucharist a celebration and a symbol of Christ's love for us."

Karen and a couple of others in the class quickly said, "Yeah, that's what I think. Yeah, me too." Other kids in the class simply nodded their heads in agreement.

Crasper's face tightened and flushed. He walked over to my desk and hovered with an outstretched index finger. His voice was angry as he shook his finger at me, saying, "Milroy, you have no business calling yourself a Catholic. None of you who think the Eucharist is *just* a symbol have any business calling yourself Roman Catholics. We, as Catholics believe in the Transubstantiation. The bread and wine are transformed into the literal body and blood of Christ during the Eucharist." Crasper was clearly unnerved and headed back toward the front of the classroom.

Karen said, "The host and wine don't taste like blood or flesh."

Crasper threw his notes onto the floor. He glared furiously as he sternly said, "I want all of you to think about what you are saying. You are Catholics. You need to start acting like Catholics."

Oh, you mean good little fuckheads who never question a thing. I kept my mouth shut, though, and I sat relieved that my answer to Crasper's question had unnerved the man enough to distract him from my glassy marijuana-affected eyes. The bell rang, ending class.

Tony and Hans tackled me in the hallway. "Hey, man, are you nuts? You're gonna get us busted!" Tony said.

"That was way too close, Pat," said Hans. I lay on the floor of the hallway laughing at the close encounter with Crasper. That was the last time I smoked a joint before class. In fact, the close call with Crasper had so unnerved Tony and Hans that they never again invited me to smoke up with them at school.

Joe displayed all the fire of a budding entrepreneur. He asked me about the trip, my education, and my plans for the future. We connected as two guys searching for meaning and purpose in life. I declined Joe's offer to stay another night and accompany him to Hilton Head Island for golf the next day. I liked the idea of fostering a friendship with him, but I was still in protection mode around people. I wanted to get back on the road, back to my thoughts, and back to my search.

As we parted Joe handed me a business card and a photo of him standing next to his friend Tom, another manager of a Chart House Restaurant, in Melbourne, Florida. Joe had written on the back of the business card, "Complimentary dinner for one (or two if he finds a date) plus a cocktail." I told Joe I would do my best to deliver the photo and card and partake of the meal, which was an unexpected gift.

I left Joe's place around ten the next morning. I had trouble navigating my way out of Savannah, straying off Highway 17 for part of the way. The late night with Joe and J.R. had resulted in my feeling drained and with little energy for the bike. Warm, humid weather appeared to threaten rain. I kept riding despite a stiff headwind. Eventually the ominous clouds spilt forth refreshing drops of rain. I kept riding through the shower.

Somewhere along Highway 17, I came across a sign, "The smallest Church in the U.S.A." Spanish Moss drooped from surrounding trees. I leaned my bike against the large sign and read:

"Memory Park Christ's Chapel. Erected in 1950 by Agnus C. Harper and in 1967 deeded to Jesus Christ. Custodian Rev. George W. Ward. Maintenance and upkeep provided by volunteers under the supervision of a committee appointed by the McIntosh Chamber of Commerce. Visitors Welcome. Sign donated by the McIntosh Chamber of Commerce."

I looked up at the wooden cross at the top of the peaked, green, shingled roof. The whitewashed, non-denominational church beckoned me in. *I want to talk to You again.* I opened the brown door and entered. The wooden floor creaked under my weight. The air inside the church was heavy and stagnant with a rich wood odor. I sat in one of the wooden chairs and tried to pray. *Nothing.* The air in the little church held a sickly sweet dankness. I walked out, mounted the bicycle, and cycled away, frustrated at my inability to pray. The little church was as empty as I was.

The visitor's center in Brunswick, Georgia recommended I stay in the *Hostel in the Woods*, just south of Brunswick. The rustic hostel was in a plush forest with towering trees dripping with Spanish moss. Beth, a young blonde girl, pedaled her bike onto the hostel property shortly after my arrival.

"Hello there, fellow bike tourist." I offered her a welcoming smile. "I'm Pat. Where are you coming from, and where are you going?"

"Hi. I'm Beth," she said with a hesitant smile. "I started in Massachusetts at my Mom's and I hope to make it to my Dad's place in Arizona." She looked sad.

"Wow, that's quite a trip." I responded.

"What? You don't think a girl can make a journey like that."

"No, that's not what I meant."

"I'm sorry. A lot of people have told me not to do this trip, and that I will not be able to make it all the way to Arizona."

"Well, Beth, you've come this far. I have no doubt that you'll make it." I looked at her bike with bulging panniers and various other items precariously bungeed to the outside. "Hey, Beth, I've been on the road awhile too, and I've found it easier to travel by organizing my gear. Want some help organizing yours?"

"There's nothing wrong with the way I pack my bike."

"Sorry, Beth. I didn't mean anything by offering to help. Maybe I'll see you later?"

"Yeah, maybe."

I began to walk away. I felt bad for having made such a stupid offer to Beth. *She's going through a tough time in her life. She must be sorting through her own issues. Maybe it has to do with her parents living apart.* I wished I could have connected to her better, simply because she was a fellow traveler. *What a presumptuous fool I've been. That's me, always looking for a way to help, to care, to befriend – using my caring nature to keep from working through my own shit. Not everyone wants to be helped, cared for, or befriended.*

I was up early the next morning despite toying with the idea of staying another night. I walked out into the morning air and there was Beth packing her bike. We had breakfast together, made small talk, and exchanged addresses. She headed off quickly after breakfast.

Beth struck me as being fiercely independent. As she pedaled away on her journey, I prayed a silent prayer of protection for her.

The traffic was light as I headed down the highway. The bike felt as if the tires weren't touching the ground. I was flying, and there was no stopping at a church today.

XI
Snowbird on Wheels

²⁹ Are not two sparrows sold for a copper coin? And not one of them falls to the ground apart from your Father's will. ³⁰ But the very hairs of your head are all numbered. ³¹ Do not fear therefore; you are of more value than many sparrows.
Matthew 10:29 NKJV

In no time I was at the Florida border. *Another milestone.* I dismounted from my bike and walked it over to the large "Welcome to Florida" sign. I took a photo of the bike leaning against the sign. *I'm already in Florida. Where are my answers to life's questions?* I mounted the bike again and headed through welcomed rain showers that cut the heat of the day as I headed for Jacksonville. After a ferry ride across the St. John's River, I found the tropical-looking Kathryn Abbey Hanna Park located on the ocean.

I tried to keep my mind busy by reading pamphlets revealing the Park's uniqueness, which included almost five-hundred acres of mature Florida coastal hammock. Hardwood trees, some of which dripped with silvery green moss, palm trees, shrubbery, and vines combined in a unique, diverse, and delicate ecosystem surrounded by wetland. After unpacking the bike and putting up my tent, I set out for a walk in the park.

I walked out to the beach and sat on the soft, warm sand. *Keep busy. Don't cry. There's nothing you can do about what happened.* My efforts to repress memories made for a fatiguing buzz in my head preventing me from really relaxing. I retreated to my tent and, despite the noise being produced by adjacent campers, I fell asleep to the sound of waves crashing on the beach. It was dark and quiet when I woke from a light slumber, disrupted by the memory of the Demon Beast sodomizing me. *It didn't happen. It didn't happen.* Eventually I drifted off again.

I left the campground and headed south along Highway A1A. The wind was at my back, the air warm, and the sky shimmered blue with a not-too-hot sun. With the ocean just a glance to my left, I concluded the day could not be more perfect. *Focus on the cycling. Focus on the scenery. It didn't happen. It didn't happen.*

It was Sunday morning. *I won't be going to church unless one reaches out and slaps me across the face.* A mere five hundred or so feet along Highway 1, I looked at the only sign along that stretch of road, "Catholic Church of the Epiphany." Okay, I'll only go to church if there's a restaurant nearby and I have enough time to eat before Mass starts. As I pedaled toward the church, I looked to the left to find "The Dutch Treat Restaurant." *Okay, God, I'll have breakfast and then go to church. Maybe you've got a message in there for me.* The little Dutch restaurant made me think of my blonde, Dutch, estranged girlfriend Gerda as I ate a huge delicious breakfast of waffles.

I was expecting to find some divine message hidden in the readings or homily of the Mass. There was none. As an observer of the Mass instead of a participant, I saw the ritual as being a celebration, however dogmatic.

The priest and people attending the Mass seemed a bit standoffish. *Do I have waffle whipped cream on my face?*

Were the sign and then the restaurant just coincidences and not some divine message? I wanted a message, but perhaps no message is the message. Yes. The Catholic Church doesn't own the message. I wish I had someone I could trust to talk to about all of this.

Cycling away from the church, I was met with a warm, stiff crosswind that tired me. My mind drifted into thoughts of sensual comfort in the face of the pain. *Will I ever be able to be intimate with a woman after what happened?* The daydream became a request. *God, send me a woman who can comfort me.* The miles passed more easily.

I rolled into the Space Center Campground in Titusville, Florida. A cooling, rejuvenating rain pelted me as I pulled in. After registering at the nearly empty campground, I chose a campsite close to the ocean but sheltered by trees. Ominous clouds were on the horizon to the east over Cape Kennedy and Merritt Island, but my tent was up before the rain saturated the ground.

I walked back toward the camp office to buy milk, cookies, and cheese, which I hoped would boost my energy. As I walked back to my tent, a beaming, thirty-three-year old, blonde-haired young woman greeted me.

"Hi. I'm Erica," she said, holding out her hand, "I wondered who I'd find camping across from me and traveling on a bike."

Is this the answer to my earlier daydream request?

"Hi, Erica. I'm Pat." She listened intently as I gave her the highlights of my trip. I listened as she explained that this campground was a favorite of hers. Although hailing from Wisconsin, Erica was in Florida working as a chef on a corporate yacht docked in Fort Lauderdale.

"Pat, there's still enough light in the day. Do you want to drive over to Merritt Island to join me for some birding?" Being a chef was Erica's job, but I soon learned birding was a passion for her.

"Sure, sounds great!" I replied. We took the short drive to Merritt Island. Black Point Wildlife Drive was a seven-mile, one-way road within the Merritt Island National Wildlife Refuge. Most of the natural salt marshes had already disappeared through coastal land development. The habitats of birds, fish, and mammals were being encroached upon in the name of progress. NASA, the owner of the land, worked jointly with the U.S. Department of the Interior's Fish and Wildlife Service to provide the refuge. A remarkable diversity of creatures was surviving in and because of the refuge.

I immediately spotted a large bird standing in shallow water.

"Hey, Erica, there's a Great Blue Heron."

"So you have been birding after all." She smiled.

"Not really. I just know the names of some of them."

"Okay, Pat. Tell me what distinguishes that bird from any other bird."

"Well, first is size, and then I also recognize its color pattern and its shape."

"Excellent. You're a birder in the making. That's what birding is all about: identifying features such as size, general shape, beak shape, and tail shape. Once you learn general features, then you can concentrate on more subtle difference such as rump patches, crests, wing bars, eye rings, stripes, field marks, tail patterns, and behaviors. Do you know the name for the study of birds?"

"Ornithology." Erica looked surprised at my answer. "No big deal. I paid attention in biology class."

"I'm impressed, Pat. Most people don't know that word."

"Erica, don't be too impressed, I don't know what a 'rump patch' is."

Revealing her slender soft neck, she threw her head back with a giggle. "That's the area between the body of the bird and the tail of the bird,"

I was amazed at the scope of her knowledge, as she identi-fied birds by sound, size, color and/or beak shape. We stayed on the island until well after sunset.

The ride to and from the island was a treat after the hun-dreds of miles I had pedaled by bicycle. From the island we headed to a Chinese restaurant. Erica enjoyed a spicy grouper fish and I had a spicy Mongolian Chicken. Erica bragged about my trip to the Chinese waitresses serving us. They seemed fas-cinated, and then excused themselves to disappear into the kitchen. Within a few minutes a graying Chinese gentleman, one of the cooks, emerged.

Bowing at Erica and me he said, "Very pleased to meet you. You travel all the way from Canada by bicycle? You very brave; that a very long way. I use live in Toronto. You know Toronto?"

"Yes, I know Toronto," I said. "My family lives in St. Thomas, which is just west of..."

"I know St. Thomas too, I been there," he quickly wiped his hands on his apron and shook my hand. "It is very nice to meet you. You enjoy the food?"

"Yes, delicious."

Erica said, "The grouper was fantastic."

"I very happy you enjoy. Nice meet you. Nice meet you." He shook his head in affirmation and smiled.

"Nice meeting you too," Erica and I said in unison, as he bowed and then disappeared into the kitchen.

"Well, Pat, it looks like you're a celebrity here," said Erica. We both laughed.

After dinner we bought some *Hagen Daz* Rum-and-Raisin ice cream, Erica's favorite. Back at the campsite she was quick to offer me another invitation.

"Pat, come on over for a beer."

"Thanks, Erica. I'd love a beer and more of your company."

We continued talking over beer and a campfire. She looked up at the now starlit night. Erica had been sitting in a comfort-able camp chair. "Pat, do you mind if I sit closer to you?"

"Not at all, Erica," I responded, tapping the top of the picnic table I was sitting on. *What am I doing? Am I ready for this?* The night air was cool as the fire burnt into embers. Our thighs touched. Our shoulders rubbed. I put my arm around Erica's shoulder. My heart was pounding. *She wants me.* I could not believe this was happening. "Erica, part of me wants to kiss you, and part of me is twisted up in the turmoil of my last relationship."

Erica calmly got up and threw another couple of pieces of wood on the fire. "Tell me what happened, Pat," she said as she sat back down. I shared my hurt and pain over the broken relationship with Gerda. *Don't tell her anything about the Demon Beast. Tell no one.*

"Pat, I know you're hurting. Sometimes you just have to move on to really let go." I could feel her desire for me in her words. I was conflicted between my feelings for Gerda and the strict code of abstinence imparted to me by the church and my parents. I was in deep fear of intimacy with any woman.

"Do you not find me attractive?" Erica asked.

"Erica, you're beautiful. I'm just too confused up here," pointing to my head. She leaned over and gently kissed me on the cheek.

"Well, okay." There was an empty pause between us. "Hey do you want to go birding with me tomorrow again?" She beamed a lovely smile that could not be refused.

"I'd love to join you." We hugged and retreated to our respective tents.

I lay in the quietness of my thoughts with the waves crashing on shore behind my campsite. Am I nuts turning down the advances of this woman? *Remember, this is what I wanted earlier in the day.*

After leaving the Roman Catholic Church I had redefined my values and beliefs regarding sexuality. *Without a commitment such as marriage, sex could be exciting, challenging and in a sense possessing a special freedom. But sex can also be detrimental to a relationship. People can just use each other under the pretense of love. So many guys at school just use their girlfriends for sex, regardless of the consequences. Why am I so different? Sex within a marriage would not be immune to becoming loveless. The commitment of marriage offers no consolation. People can be devastated by sex, and even feel trapped because of the marriage commitment.*

My requirements for sex included some high-minded prerequisites such as mutual understanding, openness, honesty, patience, unselfish giving, and mutual respect. Love was of course the most important. Marriage for me was not necessary for love, mutual respect, openness, honesty, or patience.

There it is. Sex for me is permissible within the confines of a relationship where there is love. That was my answer to the Erica dilemma. As attracted to Erica as I was, and as well as we seemed to connect, I was not in love with her.

I drifted off to sleep knowing I was at least true to this, my own defined morality. The rationalization served a deeper purpose though. I was terrified of the potential of sexual intimacy with anyone. I kept my mind busy with any thought but that of my experience at Sleepy Hole Campground. *It didn't happen. It didn't happen.*

I was already stirring from light sleep when I heard Erica's soft footsteps early the next morning.

"Hey Pat, are you ready for some more birding?"

"Absolutely, Erica. I'll be right out."

We arrived on the island at first light. Erica pulled the car to a quiet stop.

"Pat, look over there," she said, pointing to a large bird standing on a petrified tree limb jutting from the water. The black bird with its distinct orange throat stood motionless with its wings outstretched.

"That bird is called a Double-crested Cormorant. It holds that pose to dry off its wings, which aren't completely waterproof. They pose like that after they've been diving for fish."

The sunrise was spectacular, as light filtered through some big puffy clouds on the eastern horizon. Erica rolled the car along a bit further. A large, long-necked, long-legged white bird was wading through the water. "Do you know the name of that one?" Erica asked.

"I think it's an Egret."

"Very good, Mr. Smarty pants. It's actually a Great Egret."

"I've only heard of 'Snowy Egrets,' Erica. What's the difference?"

"They're both white, and they both have long black legs, but the Snowy is a bit smaller, has a shorter neck and yellow feet."

"Wow, Erica, you know your birds!"

She slowly drove a bit farther and then stopped near some wild shrubbery growing close to the dirt road. "Did you know, Pat, we can even identify birds without seeing them. Roll down your window. I'll turn the engine off. Pay attention to that shrubbery."

I listened intently and heard a "mew, mew, mew" coming from the shrub.

"Pat, what do you suppose that bird's name is?"

"Maybe it's called a 'Cat Bird.'"

"You got it! Let's sit quiet and see if we can spot one." Erica was thrilled to be with someone interested in her passion.

The birds we saw were stunning. Erica opened my eyes and ears to numerous other bird species – Glossies, Kingfishers, Grackles, Red Tailed Hawks, Ducks, Plovers, Spoonbills, Sandpipers, Loons, and Grebes. We also spotted two alligators hovering in the water with their cold eyes peering forth to ambush an unsuspecting bird.

Erica continued to comment on the different shapes of bird bills and colors, which through natural selection had evolved to serve that species in the quest for survival.

Looking at the unique shape of a Spoonbill's beak reconfirmed my view of evolution. The view taught to me by the church left little room for Darwin. I had been in high school when I had resolved this dilemma. High school science evolution was married to the Biblical story with the rationalization that God's Adam and Eve were created sometime along the revolutionary time line. The literal Creationist view of seven days was a moot point. *If we humans are indeed separate from animals by the gift of free choice and higher thought versus reaction by instinct, then that separation could have happened at any time. The Bible is full of parables. The very nature of a parable is to illustrate a spiritual truth. Why couldn't the creation story be a parable to help humans understand the power and majesty of their Creator?*

We finished birding and headed to the Space Centre for the tour I was hoping to do. The tour included the movie, "The Dream is Alive," a spectacular show about the space shuttle.

Erica and I never consummated the carnal desires we both felt. We stood amongst the towering phallic symbols of the space center's "Rocket Garden." I could feel Erica pull away in frustration. That dream was no longer alive. *At least you stuck to your convictions. How many times is a woman like Erica going to show up in your life?* Frustration welled within me because I wanted intimacy and realized Erica was a woman I could love, but I was emotionally blocked.

Back at the campsite Erica quickly packed her gear, loaded her car and after a long hug she disappeared. The campsite felt empty without her. I finished packing my gear and headed south on Highway 1 toward Melbourne.

The forty miles into Melbourne were tough. My late start meant scorching heat and a tough southwest wind to pedal against. I was relieved to make it into Melbourne and find The Chart House Restaurant.

Tom looked at me, unsure, until I produced the photo and business card from Joe. Then he burst into laughter. "This is typical of that crazy Georgia boy. Pat, come on in. We have a private function on the go tonight, but I'll seat you away from them. I hope you don't mind a limited menu, because the restaurant is closed except for this function." Tom glanced again at the back of the card, "I guess you never found a date."

"Nope." *Erica could have been my date.* "I've just been biking. Hey, Tom. I really don't need a meal from you. I just wanted to deliver the picture from Joe. Besides, I don't have any nice clothes for a restaurant like this."

"Nonsense. You pedaled your ass all the way from Canada. You're getting a meal on us." The meal of butter-fried Red Snapper, baked potato doused with sour cream and fresh ground pepper, and a tangy Caesar salad was a tasty luxury. After a thank you and a goodbye to Tom, I found a secluded spot on Melbourne beach where I could sleep. This was another way to prove I could put the Demon Beast behind me. Sleepy Hole Campground sure wasn't a safe place. *There really is no safe place in this world.*

I awoke early to find a salty mist covering my face and sleeping bag. The eastern sky over the Atlantic gradually lightened and turned various shades of pink, purple and golden yellow. The sun finally burst warm light across the horizon and into the sky.

That's it. Every day is like a lifetime. Waking is like birth. Sleep is like death. Life and everything I can pack into it is in between.

On the way out of Melbourne I headed down Highway 192 and onto Highway 92. The terrain was flat, but featured an ever-changing landscape. The temperature was in the mid-nineties. My day of cycling ended in Haines, Florida, where I camped at the Central Park Campground. I set up my tent and laid out my beach towel on the grass to continue reading *The Road Less Travelled* by Scott Peck. The title was easy for me to identify with. The bicycle tour was my way of approaching the road of life. His writing helped me redefine values and beliefs in the absence of the doctrines and tradition I had grown up with in the Catholic Church.

I sat, thinking about all of the different religions of the world. *Love was at the root of each and every one of them. Wars have been fought over religion's rituals and doctrines of supremacy, hierarchy, and exclusivity. Why does God allow different religions to flourish? Perhaps God wants us to learn to love one another despite our differences?*

Restless, I got up and took a walk around the nearly empty campground. *Is this trip really coming to an end so fast? I'm only one or two days ride from Grandma and Grandpa's place.* I pulled out my journal and listed Catholic issues I wanted to resolve through my own thinking. I used these mental gymnastics to avoid dealing with the hurt I was repressing.

Roman Catholics are known the world over for their definite anti-abortion, pro-life stance. I contemplated the issue. *As a man, I believe I have no right to tell a woman not to have an abortion.* My knowledge of physiology however, caused me to respect the sanctity of life at conception. *If a man and woman are going to consummate any relationship with a sexual union, then they should be prepared to accept conception as a consequence of that union.*

I accepted that most pro-choice advocates would react to my view with anger. They would hurl their "What about a rape victim?" argument at anyone with a pro-life stance. It was that argument that made me especially empathetic with any woman who had been raped. *Is the abortion of an innocent baby justified in the case of rape? Does the harm of rape supplant the innocent baby's right to life? No woman should have to face the emotional turmoil of such a decision.* Despite my pro-life stance, I could never throw my resolution in the face of a rape victim. *I know what it is like to be raped. It didn't happen. It didn't happen.* A wave of nausea passed through me.

My conclusion was the opposite of the Catholic Church's longstanding doctrine on birth control. *If God had created pleasure and ecstasy in the sexual union, then restricting that union to procreation was incongruent with God's nature.*

Birth control within the confines of a relationship between a man and a woman who are willing to accept the responsibility of sexual union should be encouraged, not condemned.

I contemplated the different types of birth control and understood the church's conclusion that birth control and sexual freedom undermine traditional family values. One type of birth control encouraged within the Catholic Church, though, is the Billing's Method. This method measures physiological changes in the women's body to identify the best time of the month to procreate.

The method is also popular however, among couples wanting to sexually recreate with a limited risk of conception. The Vatican's permission of the Billing's method struck me as hypocrisy. *A man's hormonal levels and libido do not fluctuate to any great degree. However, at the very time of the month when a woman is at peak sexual desire because of her hormones, she is required to abstain to prevent conception. Seems like patriarchal B.S.*

I had fervently studied the words of every chapter of Peck's book until I came to the chapter entitled "Grace." The word had very little meaning for me. *I turned from that Grace in those Virginia woods.* Somewhere I had been taught that Grace was unmerited favor from God. *This doesn't fit my resolve to live life on my own terms.* I blinded myself to the Christian reality of God's Grace through the life, death, and resurrection of Jesus Christ.

XII
Honor Your Grandparents

[1] Rebuke not an older man, but exhort him as a father, younger men as brothers,
[2] older women as mothers, younger woman as sisters, with all purity.
1 Timothy 5:1-2 NKJV

On October fifteen I cycled from Haines City to the home of my maternal grandparents, Pat and Blanche Flaherty, who lived in a mobile home retirement park in Largo, Florida. As I left central Florida and neared the Tampa/St. Petersburg area, the traffic of tractor-trailer trucks, vans, and cars passed me with disdainful energy. Soot and dust blown around by the vacuum of air from their passing stung my eyes. Clearly this was not a bicycle-friendly part of Florida. There was rarely a shoulder to ride on. My senses were on extra-high alert as I navigated my way.

My sister Callie was visiting Grandma and Grandpa, helping them to finish unpacking from their recent move. Their eighty-plus years of life had resulted in many boxes that to the untrained eye were sheer clutter and junk. Callie demonstrated a level of patience I believed few others in our family could muster, as she assisted Grandma with organizing, sorting and occasionally letting go of stuff. Grandpa would simply sit in his recliner chair with a Rosary wrapped around his hand, prayer cards and tumbler of brandy on the end table next to him.

They knew I was on the road, but had no idea when I would arrive. They welcomed me warmly.

Some of my earliest memories of my Grandma Blanche were of their 707 Harriet Avenue home in St. Paul, Minnesota. Mom, Dad, and I lived in the basement apartment of that home until I was four. During evenings I was often in their front television room, where I experienced firsthand Grandma's soft spot for Lil' Joe on *Bonanza* and Grandpa Joe on *Petticoat Junction*. Grandma seemed to delight in my singing "Tiny Bubbles" along with the *Lawrence Welk Show*. I was rewarded by being invited to climb on her lap for a sip of her brandy and water. If Grandma left the room I would then make my way to Grandpa's lap for a sip from his glass.

Grandma was a staunch Roman Catholic matriarch. As a younger homemaker in Duluth, Minnesota, she had helped her young family make ends meet by doing laundry. The carefully washed, ironed and folded clothing, vestments, and altar linens for Father Patrick and Father Terence of St. Clements Catholic Church were sacred. Blanche Flaherty viewed the work as privileged service, and the two priests were at her dinner table for home-cooked meals on a weekly basis. With the skill of a professional seamstress, she made white shirts and communion dresses for underprivileged Duluth children making their first Holy Communion.

Grandma Blanche was obviously well versed in the Catholic Papacy. She had named mom Callista. Pope Callistus I, the sixteenth in the chronology of the papacy, and later canonized a Saint, reigned from 217-222. Early Roman Catholic Popes came from diverse backgrounds, and lands such as Greece, Syria, and Africa, reflected the universality of the Church. Pope Callistus I was once a slave. *Hmmm. Having pretty much single-handedly raised us six kids, Mom was pretty aptly named.*

I was about eight years old when I received a telephone call from Grandma saying a pair of robins had built their nest in the front-yard Maple tree.

"Patrick, I know you love to climb in that tree, but you can't this spring."

"Why, Grandma?"

"There's a beautiful Mother Robin with a nest in the tree. If you climb up there and leave your scent, the Robins will kick the eggs out of the nest."

I was headstrong and curious. During the very next visit, I climbed the tree. My sister Callie, sixteen months younger, looked on.

"Pat, Grandma said not to climb the tree."

"It's okay. I know what I'm doing. The Robin won't notice my scent 'cause I'm picking up the eggs with a leaf, not my fingers."

"You better not, or I'm telling on you."

"Come on, Callie, I know you want to see the eggs as much as I do."

My attempt at concealing my scent from the Robins did not work. The next day I received a telephone call from Grandma.

"Patrick, don't lie to me. I know you touched the Robin's eggs. The Robins kicked the eggs out of the nest. The baby birds are dead."

I cried. The next time I saw Grandma I was a bit afraid of her wrath, but she had obviously detected my pain. My fear was met with her softly speaking of the incident, allowing me to apologize again, and then wrapping a loving, heavily freckled arm around my shoulders.

The end result of the baby-bird incident was my newfound respect for God's creation. I learned the respect, however, had its limits for my Irish Catholic Grandma. I showed her a freshly caught Garter Snake writhing about in my hands.

"Patrick, where did you get that dirty thing?"

"Over there in your garden." I pointed toward her blooming Peonies.

"Patrick, get rid of it. Yuk! It's a sign of the Devil."

Grandma's refrigerator was filled with mysterious little packages. Years later, during a visit to their Florida home, I finally solved the mystery. After we had dined at the local Shoney's Restaurant, I was helping Grandma to lie down in her bed for a catnap. As she undressed I saw two ketchup packs, one mustard pack, and two jam packs fall from her sleeves.

"Grandma!"

Grinning, she gave her bra a quick shift causing one more ketchup pack, plus a tartar sauce pack, to fall on the floor. I stood in a state of bewilderment.

"You never know when these can come in handy."

Grandma had seen family and friends and struggle through the Great Depression, and too many wars. Humbled, I understood the fear and pain that led to these loveable idiosyncrasies.

My nickname for Grandma was *Red Rock Bottom*. She was *Red* because of her fiery personality and penchant to color her hair red for as long as I can remember. She was *Rock Bottom* because of her resiliency.

After several years of my affectionately calling her Red Rock Bottom she said, "Patrick, you are the only one who can get away with calling me that." We had a mutual respect I cherished.

By Sunday, October twenty-six, my head was whirling with confusion, loneliness and a sense of being lost. I wasn't missing anyone in particular, but I did wish I could sit and have a good heart-to-heart talk with Sister Mary or Gerda. My journal had become my way of working out the issues in my head and heart, but I was too terrified to write about the Demon Beast. Even if I had a trusted confidant, I would not have been able to speak of the terrible event.

On this Sunday, though, the overcast skies and intermittent downpours seemed to match my feelings. I sat under the verandah at the pool patio of the mobile home park and noted the calmness in the warm drizzly air. I heard an occasional bird chirp above the distant whir of traffic travelling down Starkey Road. The rain was a reminder that it was time for me to cleanse my mind through the pages of my journal, but I only wrote about superficial things.

Callie and I had joined Grandma and Grandpa at church earlier in the day. I had cringed in the back seat of their big station wagon but my sister Callie had demonstrated amazing self-control as she drove and listened to their directions, advice, and arguments.

I did not have the slightest desire to attend church, but did so out of respect for my grandparents. At times I felt anger and wanted to stand up and walk out of the church. At other times I sat feeling an immense frustration about my disconnection from the church of my childhood. I sat in church as an observer, and chose the hypocrisy of participation so as to not hurt my Grandparents. The good Catholic boy was dead.

Orange Blossom Groves was on Seminole Boulevard, just a short distance from Grandma and Grandpa's. My travel funds were extremely low, so the decision to ask the owner, Dick, for a job was easy. Dick had known my grandparents as loyal customers for several years.

Dick wasn't a tall or obtrusive man, but with his salt-and-pepper hair, clean-cut beard, quick observations, and authoritarian demeanor, everyone knew he was in charge.

"So you'd like to work? How soon could you start?"

"Tomorrow." I tried to reply in a manner that would match the *no shit* personality Dick projected.

"Do you have a social security number? I do not want to be paying you under the table. Everything's above-board here. You're from Canada, from what your Grandmother tells me."

"I'm an American. I live in Canada, but I have a U.S. social security number. I'll bring it tomorrow."

"Okay, but are you sure you want to work here? The days are long. We start at 8:00 a.m. sharp, and work until 5:30 p.m. with a half hour off for lunch. You'll only be making three-fifty per hour and you'll be working six days per week.

"I can handle it. I've worked in the apple, tobacco, and pear harvests in Ontario. I'm not afraid of hard work. I need to make a few bucks to continue my trip."

"You better be right. You slack off once, and you're outta here."

"You won't be disappointed, sir."

Dick was right. The work was boring. I started the job in hopes of picking oranges. Instead I was hired as a gofer at the orange processing and retail building. Most mornings I would ride my bike to work. Grandpa would arrive before five o'clock and sit in the car, quietly reciting his prayer cards until my workday was done.

"Hey, Gramp, I don't expect you to pick me up every day," I said, while loading my bike into the rear of the big, yellow vehicle.

"Pat, this gets me out of the house, and the roads are dangerous this time of the night."

"Okay, Gramp. Thanks."

In my short time with my Grandparents, I noticed how slowly Grandpa was moving. He took naps for longer and longer periods of time. He would wake, read his prayer cards, and then drift off again. When he did rise from his easy chair, he would invariably comment on his rheumatism. "Pat, I seem to be getting weaker by the day. This getting old stuff is for the birds." His hip and knee joints were most affected, causing his walk to be reduced to a painful shuffle. Grandpa had always been a *can-do* kind of guy. Watching his body deteriorate was especially difficult for me.

I sat alone on the porch writing in my journal and wondering why we had to age at all. *Wouldn't it be wonderful to be able to live as long and full a life as you wanted, and then after being completely satisfied, just sit under a big tree in a peaceful field or on a warm sandy beach watching the sun set, and just leave your body?*

I was caught up in these romantic notions because I had read Richard Bach's books: *Jonathan Livingston Seagull* and *A Bridge Across Forever*. *Okay, God. I've had a good life on this earth amongst all you have created. Thank you, God. Now I'm ready for the next part of my journey. Take my soul and spirit, that which is the absolute me, and guide me into your presence. I love you, God.*

Robert Pirsig's book, *Zen and the Art of Motorcycle Maintenance*, was my companion during slow times at Orange Blossom Groves. Identifying with his motorcycle journey and metaphysical struggles became my escape from the monotony of the work. *Whether you're asked to sweep a floor, clean a storage area, or pack a skid with boxes of oranges, do it with the best Quality effort you can muster.*

After the first week of work I started to get to know the employees around me. I realized these people treated one another like family members, and I had become a part of that family.

Daily, I walked past tall, brown-skinned Shelley who most often worked on the conveyor belt that sorted the fruit by size, ripeness, and quality. She was a nineteen-year old Puerto Rican with long arms and legs. Her face drew long glances from me. After days of smiling at each other, I asked her to sit with me at lunch.

"I thought that you'd be asking to have lunch with me soon."
Wow. That's a good sign.

After initial banter about my trip and her life in Florida I asked, "Shelley, could we do something together after work someday?"

Her beauty masked a tough interior. "Pat, you seem like a nice guy. You don't wanna get mixed up with me. Trust me."

My brow furrowed. "Why not? I just wanna spend some time with you outside of this place."

"I know you find me good-looking, but I've been on my own since fifteen when my mom kicked me out." Her dark eyes pierced through me as she spoke.

"What about your Dad, Shelley?"

"He's an alcoholic. I ain't seen him since I was little." She paused. "Listen. You don't need the trouble I'd bring into your life. My boyfriend is in jail with a sixty-thousand-dollar bond because of coke dealing. He'll be getting at least three years." There was sternness in her voice projecting a streetwise wisdom well beyond her eighth-grade education. "If my boyfriend even knew I was talking to you, I'd be in deep shit, and he'd be want'n' to hurt you." She paused. "What would you do with me, anyway?"

"I'm just thinking we could take a walk on the beach and then have some dinner."

"Nope. No way. Sounds good, but I'm too dangerous. You need a nice girl from good parents and a good school."

I was mesmerized by her full lips, as she spoke with her distinctive South Florida Puerto Rican accent. *I'd like to kiss those lips.*

"What makes you think you know what I need?"

I wished I could take her in my arms. I wanted physical, intimate contact with her, but deep down knew I was incapable of connecting with her because of my pain.

"I just know I'm not the one for you." Shelley sat with her head down, not wanting to make eye contact with me. "I've got to get back to work."

Lunch ended, and Lorraine, who normally worked next to Shelley, pulled me aside. "Pat, you're going to her like a bee to a blossom. You've got to be careful of that one. She'll just bring trouble into your life."

I looked into Lorraine's sixty-year old eyes. They reflected maternal warmth and warning. "She's so tough, but maybe no one gives her a chance," I said.

"Pat, you've worked here for only a few weeks and Grace, Ginger, Chickey, Sue, Mary and me – we all think the world of you. We don't want to see you hurt. You've got a good future ahead. Here she comes."

I turned and saw Shelley glaring over at us. Lorraine quickly turned and walked away.

Shelley approached. "I know your talkin' bout me. Don't matter. I know they don't think much of me. I know they're tellin' you to stay away from me. They got that one right. Stay away from me, Pat. It's for your own good." Her voice was raised to ensure Lorraine heard. She noticed my disappointment. "Pat, forget about me. It might hurt now, but you'll get over it. You've got a good life ahead of you." Without looking back, Shelley turned and mounted the conveyor platform to sort oranges.

I walked through Orange Blossom Groves and asked the ladies if any of them needed anything lifted, pushed, stacked, or swept. Nothing. Dick was nowhere in sight to give me a task. I grabbed a broom and a shovel and headed for the parking lot. The last storm had blown sand onto the parking lot. I started sweeping in the far left section where no cars were parked. Heat beat down on me, causing me to sweat profusely.

The monotonous self-imposed task felt good as thoughts of Shelley and of Pirsig's idea of "Quality" floated through my mind. *I don't care if Dick doesn't like the fact that I'm out here sweeping his parking lot.* With the utmost attention to detail, I pushed the broom, piled and scooped the sand for over two hours. Then, I saw Dick marching toward me. *Oh shit! Here comes the boss.*

"Pat, how long have you been out here?" Dick had sternness in his voice.

I looked down at my watch. Looking back up at Dick, "Two hours, I came out just after lunch when I didn't know what else to do in there."

Dick did a quick survey of the area swept clean. "Ya know, we have a machine that does this sort of thing. It's over at the other location, but maybe we could get it over here for you."

"Actually Dick, thanks, but I like it out here. I like to work hard. I really don't mind doing this with a broom and shovel."

"Pat, you've proven yourself to be the hardest worker I've got. I wish I could have three of you, then I could fire ten of the lazy asses."

"Dick, I've got one question. I left my T-shirt on, but it's hot. Do you mind if I work out here with my shirt off?"

Dick grinned. I could tell he wanted to burst out laughing. "Pat, it's hotter than hell out here. Take your shirt off." He walked away. *Quality wins out again.*

The tedious, sometimes hard work made the days of the first week seem extra long. I constantly reminded myself that the work I did there was a reflection of myself. By making my work Quality work, I imagined I was reflecting attributes such as responsibility, understanding, caring, honesty, and independence. The most menial tasks became satisfying. The long days began to fly by, and one week blurred into another.

"Hey, Dick, this Saturday will be my last day of work. I've got to get back on my bike and continue the tour."

"Pat, I wish you could stay, but I know your life has better things in store for you than continuing to work here."

"Thanks, Dick."

Saturday came quickly. I began working in the produce section, when Ginger tapped me on the shoulder. "Pat, me and the girls from produce have a little goodbye gift for you. I hope it fits," she said, handing me a bright orange T-shirt.

"Wow, Ginger, I didn't expect a gift. This is great. I'm gonna miss you all."

"Pat, we want you to wear the shirt for the rest of the day. Read what we put on it."

I could feel all the eyes of the women from the produce section on me as I held the shirt up and read the inscription aloud. "I Worked So Hard, Ached So Much, Made So Little. O.B.G."

"Ain't that the truth," said Lorraine, and everyone burst out laughing.

I turned and saw Chicky beaming at me. "Pat, I got the okay from Dick, you get a twenty minute extra-long lunch today so I can cut your hair."

"Okay," I said with some hesitation. Chicky looked like a hairdresser, with her thick mane of well-kept, peroxided, sandy blonde hair pulled back and up onto her head. She had a chewing-gum smile ringed with bright red lipstick, and mascara that perfectly complemented her dark eyes.

"Don't fret, sweetie. I'm a trained hairdresser."

"Why are you working here then?"

"Fair question, Pat. I started here part time just to help out, and got to know everyone, so I stayed. This is like a family."

"Wouldn't you make more money being a hairdresser?"

"I probably could, but I like the people here, and I like doing hair just for family and friends like you."

At lunch, I sat and watched Sue receive a haircut from Chicky. Sue's long unruly hair became stylish as Chicky trimmed and teased. *Maybe she'll do okay with my hair.*

"Pat, you're up." I sat on the lunchroom chair we had placed outside. Chicky began to comb my hair. I sat enjoying feeling her hands run through my hair as I looked out into the orange groves. Chicky obviously became aware of my sensual enjoyment as her gentle hands performed the cut. "Pat, you know this is just a courteous cut as my gift to you on your last day."

"Yeah. Thanks, Chicky."

I sat grinning, with my eyes closed.

"I know you young guys can get the wrong idea when a woman starts running her fingers through your hair, but it feels good, doesn't it?"

"Feels great."

"Just you remember, I'm a married woman."

We both burst out laughing.

I never did say good-bye to Shelley. She wasn't at work on Friday or Saturday. I concluded that either she was too shy or too aloof to say goodbye. Later on I discovered that the older women had approached Dick and asked her to be transferred to the other location, all for my "benefit."

Jean Cameron was a reporter for the Seminole-Largo Beacon. She knocked on Grandma and Grandpa's door late one afternoon to ask if she could write a story about my trip. A few days before, Dad had called. He had asked me if I wanted a reporter to contact me about my successful bike trip from Ontario to Florida.

"No, Dad. I don't need anything like that. Thanks for the offer, though."

Despite my resistance, Grandma had contacted the paper upon Dad's prompting.

The reporter, Jean, carefully listened to me recount the route and highlights. "Pat, the trip sounds amazing, but I'm interested in knowing why you took it."

I paused for quite some time, searching for the words.

"If it's too personal, and you can't share, that's okay."

"No, Jean. I don't mind sharing. I'm just wondering where to begin."

Jean had an intuition that her journalistic integrity and curiosity showed. "Did the trip have anything to do with a girlfriend?"

I blushed at her bull's-eye question. "Yeah, it did, Jean. We were engaged. We met at University. I broke off the engagement. Now I miss her and think I made a mistake."

"Pat, that happened to a friend of mine. Give yourself time to heal. The trip was a great idea. You seem like a great guy. Don't worry, you'll find the right one."

I paused at her comments. My mind whirled with thoughts of the Demon Beast, Gerda, Tamara, Erica, and Shelly. *What will my future hold?*

"Was there any other reason for your trip?"

"Well, Jean, I guess I'm trying to decide what I want to do in life. I thought about being a chiropractor, medical doctor, or physiotherapist. I am leaning toward becoming a chiropractor. I want a health-care profession where I can help people and work with my hands."

"Why chiropractic, Pat?" Jean asked.

"When I was sixteen years old, I was playing senior level basketball at St. Joseph's High School in St. Thomas, Ontario. I injured my back and hip at the time. Mom took me to the family doctor, who wanted to put me on painkillers and anti-inflammatory drugs. Mom had been seeing a chiropractor at the time for a whiplash injury. She knew that drugs would just mask the problem, and so she took me to her chiropractor.

"The chiropractor took the time in doing his history and examination to figure out I had a huge muscle imbalance due to practicing lay-ups off my right leg because of being left-handed. I was out of pain after one treatment, and he explained that I had to practice the lay-ups on the opposite side. Chiropractic got at the problem instead of just masking symptoms, so I was impressed."

Jean scribbled a couple of notes and looked at me with penetrating eyes. "Pat, you're the kind of guy who will be successful in whatever you decide to do."

"Thanks, Jean."

"I think I have enough for an article about your trip. Do you mind if I snap a picture of you?"

"Not at all. Maybe you could take a picture of me standing next to my bicycle."

"That's a great idea. You've been so gracious sharing what has obviously been a very personal journey. I am deeply grateful. People will like learning about this trip."

Jean did write the article, entitled "Snowbird on Wheels."

After the interview and photograph, Grandpa and I drove to the Greyhound bus terminal where I dropped off an army duffle bag stuffed with clothes, a photo album, and other mementos I had collected. The bag was quite heavy, but it cost me less than ten dollars to have it sent on to the Greyhound terminal in Fort Lauderdale.

"Grandpa, I'm feeling pretty confused about my life. I was hoping to find some answers on the trip, especially about Gerda. I love her but don't seem to be able to commit to her."

"Pat, can I give you some advice?" Grandpa asked as we drove from the terminal.

"Gramp, you can say anything to me."

"I think you should go back to Ontario, fix things up with Gerda, and get married. Go off and elope if you want to. The two of you could come down here to honeymoon if you want."

I felt loved by Gramp and appreciated his heartfelt recommendations. His blue-collar pragmatic response was not the wisdom-filled answer I sought, but I loved him for it. I loved him because he spoke practical words from his heart.

"Thanks, Gramp."

In truth, connecting with anyone, Gerda, Erica, or Shelley, on a deep emotional or physical level, was beyond me. The effort at repressing what had happened made me wall myself off from everyone, including family and close friends.

Thanksgiving was a good day to leave. The traffic was very light, and Highway 60 sported a good shoulder most of the way. My thoughts were with Grandma and Grandpa. I spoke silent words to God thanking Him for my grandparents who had graciously fed and sheltered me during my stay. I empathized with the loneliness that I imagined would creep back into their lives as I left. I was glad they had each other.

I was meditating on the notion of giving thanks as I pedaled along. I entered into a dreamy state with the rhythm of the pedal stroke.

"Pat, don't end your trip. Keep cycling." The Voice was strong, quiet, and peaceful.

I tried to ignore the Voice.

"Pat, turn around." My mind raced through my plans: get back to school, graduate, become a chiropractor, get back together with Gerda, get married, have a family.

"Pat, turn around. Continue your trip."

After eighty-five miles I pulled into Lake Wales Campground. The campsite was nearly filled because of the annual migration of snowbirds from the northern States and Canada. No one came to befriend me, offer me a place at their table, share a meal, or tell stories of travel and adventure. I sat at the picnic table and then lay in my tent with a weighty discontent.

"Turn around. Don't end your trip," the powerful, soft Voice again whispered.

Is this God speaking to me? Is this my own intuition? Is there any difference between my inner intuition and God's voice? At the Forest Tabernacle, I had emphatically told our Lord that I was doing things in my life my way. The Lord had told me He was with me anyway. I had reaffirmed my decision to continue the trip on to Fort Lauderdale, fly home and return to school.

Lying in my tent, I spoke softly back to God. "You created me. You created this world. If You did send Jesus to the earth to live as a human, and Jesus and You are One, then by denying Jesus have I denied you?" My throat tightened a bit. I continued speaking to God, "I believe in You, God, I just can't give my life to Jesus, because I have to live my life my way."

"Pat, don't end the trip. Turn around."

I drifted into a fitful sleep after reciting the only prayer I could continue to believe in – *The Lord's Prayer.*

"Our Father Who art in heaven, hallowed be Thy name, Thy kingdom come, Thy will be done, on earth as it is in heaven. Give us this day our daily bread and forgive us our trespasses, as we forgive those who trespass against us. And lead us not into temptation, *but deliver us from evil...*"

XIII
Deliver Me from Evil

¹⁴ Do not enter the path of the wicked,
And do not walk in the way of evil.
¹⁵ Avoid it, do not travel on it;
Turn away from it and pass on.
¹⁶ For they do not sleep unless they have done evil;
And their sleep is taken away unless they make some-
one fall.
Proverbs 4: 14-16 NKJV

Cars sped by me as the dense morning fog burned off. On several occasions, shouted insults rang from the passing vehicles,
reminding me that, as a bicyclist, I was invading their roadway.

"Get off the road, you fucking idiot. Where do you think
you're going, stupid asshole?"

The comfortable shoulder of Highway 60 had given way to
only two lanes of heavy truck traffic.

"Pat, turn around. Don't end your trip," whispered the soft
inner Voice. "Pat, turn around." The Voice was disrupted by
the blast of a truck horn. The eighteen-wheeled giant passed
within inches of my shoulder. I braked, veering off the pavement into quack grass and sand. My legs shook. I coasted to a

stop, gathered my wits, and then pedaled back onto the road. The white strip of paint marking the edge of the road became my sole point of concentration. Like a tightrope walker, I held the front wheel over the ribbon of white, pedaling and telling myself this would protect me from the traffic passing all too close for comfort.

"Pat, turn around."

No. I am not afraid. I ignored the Voice and continued pedaling, despite hurled insults and close calls with trucks. After about thirty miles the landscape gradually changed. Carefully maintained orange groves gave way to rugged swampland and fields of scrub brush. With over fifty miles to cover before reaching the east coast at the end of Highway 60, I wondered if I would see any more civilization.

Finally, a gas station! I purchased water and filled my bottles to an aloof reception from the gas station's attendant.

"Are their many more gas stations down the road?" I smiled at the man, hoping for a friendly response.

"Nope," he replied, with a squinting right eye and furrowed brow, as he glanced over my shoulder, resting his gaze on my bicycle. He turned away rapidly.

I pedaled on. The hot air was stifling, heavy with humidity. The traffic that plagued me earlier was now gone. I was alone. The world seemed to hold me in a foreboding quietness. I searched the sky for a sign of an impending storm. Nothing. There was nothing. No cars, no trucks, nothing for miles.

Then – Two men in a small sandy clearing.

Leaning against an old, green, dented pickup truck, they were guzzling bottles of beer. I felt their eyes follow me as I approached at a steady pace. I offered them a friendly nod. My gesture was met with cold stares. I pedaled on.

A couple of miles later I heard the truck approaching. *Oh shit, here it comes.* The truck slowed. Hard-driving rock music blared from open windows. The man on the passenger side was sitting on the window-ledge with his legs in the truck. "Git it lit, man," the driver shouted. They broke into a chorus of whooping and hollering. The man's hands worked feverishly on top of the truck. Something sparked. He made a tossing motion toward me.

The world slowed. *Bang!* Bright, blinding light.

The explosion was near the back of my head. Every bone in my body rattled. The bicycle frame vibrated with fury, hurting my hands. I was instantly blinded, instantly deafened. Somehow I remained conscious. I gripped the bars of my bike and coasted to a stop. My body began to shake uncontrollably as I pulled my feet from the toe clips and found footing on solid ground.

Burnt powder hung in the air.

Extreme fatigue hit my body. I stood shaking and holding the bicycle. *Please, not blindness, please, not deafness.* Intuitively I knew the cowards had sped off. I was alone. I was deaf, blind, shaking.

I opened my eyes hoping for something other than blackness.

Nothing, for what seemed an eternity.

Slowly, ever so slowly, I began to see glimmers of light. A mosaic of innumerable black and white spots gave way to a tunnel of vision. I closed my eyes again, trying to steady my breathing, but my heart pounded. I opened my eyes, and the tunnel vision finally gave way to full vision.

I looked behind me. The two-lane road was empty. I turned and looked ahead. Nothing. I tried to make myself stop shaking, but the effort made me shudder convulsively. Because of my exercise physiology studies, I knew what was happening: a massive sympathetic nervous system response. This was the fight-or-flight response. I knew it would pass. Pedaling the bicycle would be the best way to tame the sympathetic response. The exercising muscles would call upon already racing cardiovascular and respiratory systems.

Sticking my fingers in my ears and tugging on my lobes made no difference to the *whish* and *whir* deafness filling my head. I tried to speak, but could not hear the sound of my own voice.

Placing my shaking right foot into the toe clip, and, with a few pushes on the pavement from my left foot, I started to coast. My arms shook uncontrollably as I attempted to bear my upper body weight on the handlebars. I quickly grasped for the brake levers and stopped the bike. I was still too weak.

Are those guys coming back? Maybe I could retreat to the swamp for safety? Shit. There's gators in there. Maybe I'll find a farmer tending to his orange groves. Shit. Those guys could be the farmers!

Okay, I think I can pedal now. I pushed the bike along to a coast. My body continued to shake. Shifting into lower gears, I made wobbly childlike pedal strokes and then headed east down that desolate stretch.

I longed for a passing Patrol car. *Someone please stop and help me! Where was the still quiet Voice now?* Nothing. I had to help myself. There was no time for self-pity. I had to take charge of the situation.

Despite profound fatigue, I continued to pedal on, but after the explosion, it took hours to travel just a few miles. My destination was Vero Beach on the Atlantic coast. I considered finding a spot to pitch my tent and rest amongst the passing swamp and brush land, but the thought of being alone or, worse, those guys finding me, made me continue. The effort of pedaling was so extreme, at times I groaned out loud, only to be met with the silence of my deafened state. I longed to see a mileage marker, a sign, a gas station, but there was nothing for mile after mile.

Hours passed. The whir and whoosh in my head gave way to a constant ringing buzz. *Maybe I won't be permanently deaf after all.*

I shouted as loud as I could. "Hey, hey, hello, I'm here. I want to hear." Nothing registered. A few miles later, I tried again, "Here, hear, here... I want to hear." *Yes.* I registered faint muffled words beneath the ringing buzz. I pedaled past a couple of empty crossroads. Next was an overpass. Then I coasted into the sanctuary of a gas station with a variety store attached.

"How much further to Vero Beach?" I asked the clerk.

"Oh, you got about nine more miles." I had to concentrate very hard to hear her muffled response in my improving yet still deafened state.

"Thanks," I said, turning and heading out of the store to stand next to my bike. I ate a couple of bananas and drank a quart of orange juice. I contemplated another nine miles.

Under normal circumstances, this distance would have been a sheer pleasure to cycle. Now? As the sun lowered in the western horizon, I dreaded even the next mile. I pulled out my map and looked at the location of campgrounds. The closest was eight miles north of Vero Beach. Seventeen more miles would be impossible. I decided just to get to Vero Beach and then seek shelter.

One thing at a time. Back on the bike. One pedal stroke after another. One landmark after another. Come on, Pat. Keep the pedals turning. Only eight miles to go.

Dusk had come when I finally reached Vero Beach. I cycled toward the beach, the boardwalk, and civilization. People milled about everywhere. Couples walked arm in arm. Beachgoers headed to vehicles. Groups of youth huddled together. Surfers walked with their boards under their arm. I wanted someone friendly to notice me. No one did. I walked my bike along the sidewalk adjacent to the beach. The place seemed foreign to me. I felt as though I was there, but not there.

Again I pulled out the map, and along with it my campground guidebook. There was nothing close. Every motel and hotel I looked at had a neon sign, "No Vacancy."

Hmmm. Well okay, I've slept on the beach before. I'll just have to do it again. Overcome the fear. Overcome the memory of the night of terror. I mounted. Riding south, I turned into the first oceanfront subdivision. Weaving my way down streets, I found a public access to the beach.

Walking my bike along the wooden access ramp, I approached the promise of rest. The weight of the bicycle caused the skinny rear wheel to sink into the sand. *Stop. Don't get sand in the chain. Muster more energy.*

I carried the bike. Leaning it against the wood railing of the ramp, I pulled off the panniers and sleeping bag. *Lock the bike to the wood railing. Okay. You're safe now.* I pulled off my shoes and socks. I twisted my feet into the soft, still warm sand and gave a heavy sigh at this bit of comfort.

I spread out the sleeping bag, sat and watched the last of the die-hard surfers come in, as the ocean and sky slipped into inky darkness. I gazed at the bicycle ten feet away. The rhythmic sound of the waves calmed me.

I had ignored the still quiet Voice, the Voice of shelter, the Voice of safety, the Voice of protection. There are consequences of ignoring that Voice. The past day bore witness to those consequences. I had pedaled away from hell.

XIV
Vero Beach Rendezvous

¹⁶ The people who sat in darkness have seen a great light, and upon those who sat in the region and shadow of death Light has dawned. ¹⁷ From that time Jesus began to preach and to say, "Repent, for the kingdom of heaven is at hand."
Matthew 4:16-17 NKJV

In the distance I could hear the voices and music of a party at one of the beachfront homes. A starry night filled the sky as I lay back on the sleeping bag. Exhausted, I drifted off to sleep.

At two in the morning I woke to voices on the street adjacent the dune. Within a few minutes, the soft padding of footsteps approached the wooden ramp and stairs. I squinted into blackness toward the railing of the stairs. *Is that person looking at me?* The individual reached over the railing and touched the front tire of my bicycle. Our eyes locked.

"Is that a bicycle?" A soft voice asked, as I looked up at a woman.

"Yeah. It's a bike," I said, with hesitation in my voice.

"Are you sleeping on the beach?" My hearing was restored, yet I was still plagued by a ringing buzz.

"Well, I was trying to sleep."

"Where are you from?"

"Canada."

"Canada? You didn't ride your bike all of the way from Canada, did you?"

"Yeah. Actually I did."

A conversation between complete strangers had begun. The mention of Canada became the impetus for the stranger to continue down the steps, proclaiming with a lisp, "Hey, I'm from Canada too. My name's Danny. In fact, I am a former dancer with the Montreal Ballet." Danny slowly walked through the sand toward me.

I had never met an openly gay man before. I changed my position on the sleeping bag to a cross-legged sit, as Danny sat in the sand next to me on my left. "Did you hear the music from the house party?"

"Yeah. I fell asleep to the sounds of that party."

"I was at that party. Everyone who is anyone in Vero Beach was at that party," Danny spoke with an air of superiority. "What's your name?"

"Pat."

"Well, Pat, it is my pleasure to meet you." Danny held forth a soft, limp hand. I shook hands with him.

Please just leave me. I just want to be alone. An uncomfortable silence ensued between the two of us.

Danny broke the silence. "Aren't you lonely traveling like this?"

"No." *Come on man, get the hint. I'm not interested.*

"Do I make you nervous?"

"No." I was, in fact, very nervous and scared.

Danny shifted his body closer to me and then wiggled his buttocks into the sand in a gesture I understood and found repulsive.

"Do you want some company?" The gay stranger leaned toward me wetting his lips and softening his mouth.

"No," I said abruptly. "I was just trying to get some rest." I felt extremely uncomfortable.

"Do you sleep on the beach often?"

"Only a couple of times. Tonight when I rode into Vero Beach it was getting dark. There were no campgrounds nearby, so I found this spot on the beach."

Danny leaned toward me again, this time placing his hand on my thigh. "Pat, are you sure you don't want some company?"

"No. Please. I'm not interested. Please just leave me alone," I said. Politely but firmly I removed his hand from my thigh.

"Do you see those buildings over there?" I looked south toward the commercialized section of Vero Beach. Bright lights cut through the blackness of the night. "Those are the tallest buildings here. No one can build a building taller than that. We have rules here that must be abided by, and that includes strangers." Danny's tone changed. "You know, you are trespassing on this beach. I could easily have you arrested."

"I'll just leave, then. I had no intention of trespassing. I just wanted to be left alone to rest on this beach."

"Okay, then. What a shame. We could have had some fun together. I hope I didn't offend you."

"No, I'm not offended. Please just leave me."

"Well, okay. A real shame. Don't worry. I won't call the cops." Danny, the gay stranger, stood and walked away toward the lights of the Vero Beach boardwalk.

I sat on the beach, thankful to be alone again, yet nervous. *He wanted sex with me. Why me? I was a complete stranger to him. There's desperation in looking for sex from a stranger on the beach.*

Only the rhythmic break of waves on the beach confirmed that the Atlantic Ocean lay before me. I wanted sleep, but was afraid my privacy would again be disturbed. I sat gazing at the darkness of the ocean as long hours passed.

Finally, this night is coming to an end. The blackness hovering over the ocean lightened. Another hour passed. Through distant dark clouds, small streaks of light heralded the impending sunrise in the eastern sky.

I shook the sand from the sleeping bag, packed the bicycle, and made my way over the wooden access ramp and stairs. I quietly pedaled through the now silent beachfront community. The previous night's festivities had obviously been extinguished by exhaustion, drug-induced delirium, and carnal satisfaction, or some combination thereof.

Highway 1 South had a good paved shoulder and brought me to Hobe Sound, Florida. The ride was thankfully short. My mind and body were exhausted. I longed for the safety of a quiet campground. I pulled into Jonathan Dickinson State Park.

Another Sunday morning. I was not looking for signs telling me to attend a celebration at the next Catholic Church. The wind was strong and cycling was laborious as I left the state park. Methodically, I pumped my legs and put the miles behind me. Low ominous clouds rolled in. *West Palm Beach seems dreary. People around here look worn out, depressed. Or is it me? Keep going, Pat. Get to Fort Lauderdale. End this fucking trip, your trip, the trip you love, the trip you have come to hate. Get back to Canada, back to school, back to your life, your way.*

A flash of the terror I had experienced in Virginia struck me. *I can't handle this. It didn't happen. It didn't happen.*

I skirted the rain until Pompano. Then, heavy pelting drops fell from the sky. I sought quick shelter under a tree. The warm rain saturated my sweaty shirt, shorts, socks, and shoes. Within minutes the gutters along the roadside became rushing streams of water. *Keep going. You're already soaked.* At Fort Lauderdale, the bicycle left a wake of water and my feet were completely submerged during the down strokes. The deluge of rain overwhelmed the sewer systems, causing flooding in the lower-lying roadways.

The miles I put behind me had been ever-changing – meditative, monotonous, laborious, violent, terrifying, desperate, glorious, energizing, prayerful, dreamlike, and confirming. The yellow twelve-speed bicycle had come to feel like one of my appendages. The Still, Quiet Voice whispered once more, "Pat, don't end your trip." Disappointment accompanied my denial of that request. I was determined to go on with my life my way, and so I did.

XV
Down, Down Under and Gratitude

¹⁹ Then they cried out to the Lord in their trouble, *And*
He saved them out of their distresses.
²⁰ He sent His word and healed them, And delivered
them from their destructions.
²¹ Oh, that *men* would give thanks to the Lord *for* His
goodness, And *for* His wonderful works to the children
of men!
Psalm 107:19-21 NKJV

I completed a Bachelor and Master of Arts at the University
of Western Ontario and then, in 1994, graduated from the
Canadian Memorial Chiropractic College. Years of study confirmed my vision of being surrounded by books.

Over the years of my chiropractic practice I was in awe of
the many patients who disclosed memories of sexual abuse or
other traumas. I had compassion for these individuals because
of my own violation.

Sexual abuse causes a myriad of problems in the victim's
life. I have experienced many of the problems in my own life.
They can include shame, guilt, depression, and post-traumatic
stress disorder (PTSD). Some victims go on to suffer with ad-
dictions and suicidal tendencies. Survivors of sexual abuse also

experience difficulty in forming and maintaining relationships, and often have issues with intimacy.

My studying was a major coping strategy for me. I used the focus of my education, and then the building of my practice to keep the pain of my violation deeply repressed.

One of the reasons I thrived as a chiropractor was because of the nature of the doctor-patient relationship. Strict boundaries, trust, compassion, and consent are part and parcel to that relationship. I felt safe within those boundaries. The doctor-patient relationship helped me to heal, as well as those with physical pain that were under my care.

My shoulder was injured as I attempted an anterior thoracic adjustment to a morbidly obese, four-hundred-pound individual. This particular adjustment is performed like a bear hug with the patient face-up on the chiropractic treatment table. I tore the sternal (breast-bone) attachment of my pectoralis major (chest) muscle off my rib cage and dislocated my shoulder at the same time. I felt the shoulder go partially back into its socket, but the damage was done.

I continued to work, in spite of my injured shoulder, for over three years, which created even more damage. Lightning bolts of pain with each adjustment forced me to suspend my practice in June of 2009. A locum (fill-in doctor) took my place in my practice for three more years, and finally I sold my practice in September of 2012.

I married, had a son and divorced. I love and loved my son deeply, and didn't understand a society that devalued the role of a father in a son's life. Clutching a globe, I held my right finger on Halifax and my left finger on Brisbane. The vision regarding my son had come true. It was the fall of 2008; Sean was now living in Brisbane, Australia. I was in Halifax, Nova Scotia, at the opposite end of the earth. When I lay my head on the pillow at night, meditating on the love of Jesus heals the pain of Sean's absence.

How much pain had I inflicted on Jesus when I turned from Him that day at the Forest Tabernacle? The pain of my son's absence and the loss of my fatherly role in his life was my lesson about turning from God's grace.

For months I sat watching TV movie after movie, trying to numb the pain of my son's absence and my not working. I was grieving.

I began to remember my encounter with the Demon Beast around the time Sean moved to Australia. He was only ten when he moved there with his Mom and her husband. I think the emotional pain of Sean moving, coupled with the practice ending shoulder injury, stirred the emotional pain of the sodomy rape, and I started to remember.

The memories threw me into a sleepless depression.

I woke from a light sleep with my heart pounding remembering my tent fly being unzipped, my ankles grabbed, my violation by two men, and whatever drug they used on me. Despite the emotional turmoil, I wanted to remember more. The next night I woke and fervently wrote about waking up naked in a drugged stupor, and then being raped. On the third night I was stirred out of bed by the full memory of my desperate pleading, begging the one man whose voice I recognized, The Priest.

Flipping through the twenty-five-year old photo album of the bicycle trip, I found The Priest's prayer card I had picked up from the display table at the Retreat Center. For all those years that prayer card had rested between maps and pamphlets I had collected from the trip. On one side of the prayer card was a quote and on the other side was The Priest's name, his date of ordination, and a headshot photo.

I had a west coast baseball game on television with the volume turned nearly off as I sat in the cushy, leather recliner, with my laptop opened and the browser turned to a Google search. Next to me was a small table upon which stood a tumbler of Scotch. I picked up the tumbler of golden liquid, whiffed the pungent aroma and then took a small sip, before I entered the name of The Priest.

He had been a newly ordained Catholic Priest in 1986 and he was still a Catholic Priest in the same Arizona city. Looking up from the screen of my laptop, I checked the score of the baseball game. I took another sip of the single malt whiskey. I shed no tears over this revelation about The Priest. I had cried on the inside over the pain of the rape for over half of my life. I was suddenly struck by the clarity of what I felt toward The Priest: pity. I was not angry. I held no malice toward him.

In truth, I had been wondering if my break from the Catholic Church was because of the inherent and endemic pedophilia the church harbored. Maybe my experience with the Demon Beast that started at Sleepy Hole Campground – which I dubbed Canaan's Campground – was the evil one's final violation, as I left the cesspool of Roman Catholicism. Being raped anally – it has to be one of the worst physical and emotional degradations a man can suffer. Similarly, any church's insistence that we commune with Jesus only in their contrived fashion is one of the worst spiritual degradations man can suffer.

Too often churches rob people of a genuine and personal spiritual search through the institutionalization of the relationship with God and Christ as Savior. I now know God can reach anyone, anywhere, anytime, and shower that person with grace that is independent of a church's doctrine and ritual: in any church, in the Catholic Church, or in the woods.

After sharing with my parents what had happened with The Priest, I struggled with their unwavering devotion to the Catholic Church. Mom and Dad continued to give large sums of money to the church. Like many Catholics, they believed that pedophilia was only an isolated problem caused by a few deranged priests. There are, however so very many survivors out there, especially the childhood victims of pedophile priests.

"Dad, don't stop giving money to the Catholic Church."

"What do you mean Pat?"

"Well, Dad, it bothered me at first, but I figured out how to make it right in my heart. Don't stop giving to the Church because there's lots of abuse victims of Catholic priests out there who will need to be compensated."

When I set out on my bike tour, I wanted to know if the Jesus of my youth was real. I didn't know if I would find Him. I wanted to search under my own terms. My search for Him was distinctly different from the religious and dogmatic approaches I had grown up with.

I thought if Jesus was real, then I could find Him. My hunch was I wouldn't find Him within the walls of a church. As a kid, I spent a lot of time alone in the woods. There's purity in the woods, and I felt close to nature, God's creation, which made me think I would find Him there, but I wasn't sure.

I have concluded, that because I was seeking to know the truth about the Catholic Church, I received the answer in the worst possible way, sodomy rape.

I have come to believe some people probably have the ability to have visions about their life or the lives of others. I think the trauma of the sodomy, coupled with being drugged, allowed me to disassociate and somehow tap into that ability to see the future.

Two men raped me. They preyed upon me because I was travelling alone, but that only explains the physical manifestation of my violation, and I had lots of physical evidence the next morning. There's more to it than that. I have no doubt the Demon Beast was and is real. Evil is real. I've come to believe that the rape took place in two planes of existence. My body was raped on the earthly plane. My spirit was raped on an ethereal plane.

I was looking for truth. Was Jesus real? Was the Catholic Church a place of truth? My experiences have actually confirmed the basic tenants of Christianity, that God is a loving Creator, that this is a fallen world, that God became man in Christ Jesus, and that Jesus is a resurrected, living, and loving

Savior. I don't see any of my experience as God punishing me. I do see my story, though, as being an important one that might teach people, Christians and non-Christians, about the importance of our spiritual journey. I see my story as a way to teach people about the love and grace of Jesus.

Love is our attempt to bridge the isolation of self that each of us is born into. We all fail at loving, individually and collectively, but we all continue to hope that by overcoming our isolation, love is left triumphant in our self and in the world.

I met Jesus Christ in the Virginia woods in 1986. I sought that communion with Him. He is real. I isolated myself from Him, but He did not turn from me. My journey to healing did not begin until I welcomed Jesus back into my life. While remembering my trauma and writing this book, I realized I had maintained isolation from my Savior as I repressed the memories of being violated.

I considered all of the moments I thought perfect in my life. The intensity of my first love, the bond created as I held my newborn son for the first time, the perfection of an unblemished flower ready to bloom, the serenity of a quiet beach as I witnessed the sunset in a burst of purple and rose light beams. All of those moments paled in comparison to my experience with Jesus. The light of Jesus' love was the most intense and penetrating light I ever knew. That light emanated perfect, all encompassing, unconditional love that defies written description.

I am thankful to remember that radiant light of His love and know Jesus loves me unconditionally. Gratitude has been an important part of my healing journey.

It took a while, but I gained a sense of gratitude for my injury. I gained a state of gratitude for my first wife, Sean's Mom, and even gratitude for their move to Australia. This doesn't mean I don't miss my son, but rather I am at peace with the situation and value the special time Sean and I spend together all the more. The injury and my son's move to Australia afforded me the time to remember, write and begin the healing process.

I gained a sense of gratitude for my second wife, who gently led me back into a relationship with Jesus Christ.

My first and second marriage both ended in divorce and I fully accept my fault for the marriages falling apart. It is difficult to be married to a guy with deeply repressed wounds. Intimacy is difficult. Boundary and control issues interfere with communication, especially with your significant other. I am thankful to both of these women for being in my life, and for the life lessons I learned from them.

Gratitude even means I am thankful for the sexual assault that took place in 1986. Many people reading this will find this hard to believe. Why would anyone be thankful for something so devastating and life-influencing? Realizing the good that comes out of something bad is incredibly freeing.

Of course I would never have wanted this to happen to me, but it did. My repression forced me into continuing my education until I graduated as a chiropractor. The repression of the assault shaped the doctor of chiropractic that I became – a doctor with immense empathy for others who have survived their own physical and emotional traumas.

The assault led me on a long path back into a relationship with Jesus. I am in the relationship with Him now, that I had set out to find on that 1986 bicycle trip. *Thank you Jesus for your unconditional love.*

Acknowledgements

My first draft of the manuscript was hardly worthy of the word "manuscript!" The only structure to the story was that it followed the bicycle tour in a chronological fashion. I had not even fully recalled the sodomizing rape or who the rapists were in that first draft. It took, in fact, over 20 years for me to even mention that I had been raped to anyone, let alone write about it.

I am grateful for my friend, the poet Julia McCarthy, who read the first, very rough draft of the manuscript. Julia gave me the title, *The Forest Tabernacle* and her gentle ways of acceptance and encouragement helped me to continue with my writing and healing.

I am thankful to Blair Kenney, PhD, my first editor. The three editorial turns with Blair were remarkable learning experiences that were coupled with encouragement.

I am grateful to my parents, Don and Callista Milroy and my brother Dan and sister-in-law Kathy, brother Mark, and sisters Callie, Amy, and Sarah. Sharing the repressed memories with you was part of my healing. Each one of you gave me your loving encouragement. I have been especially blessed by the time spent with my Dad and brothers, Northern Pike and Walleye fishing the pristine waters of Manitoba—the perfect backdrop for discussing the manuscript and my healing journey.

Thank you to my sister-in-law, Kelly McMasters, author of *Welcome to Shirley: A Memoir from an Atomic Town,* which was published in 2008. The stirring rendition of her coming of age in small town Shirley, Long Island with the setting of a leaking nuclear laboratory was inspirational for my writing.

In my publisher, colleague and now friend, Dr. Elizabeth Pilicy I found a kindred spirit whose patience and encouragement brought this book to fruition.

Rev. Lennett J. Anderson, Senior Pastor of Emmanuel Baptist Church in Halifax, Nova Scotia gave me friendship and prayerful support that helped me through some dark times as I navigated life while writing the book. I will always be grateful to Pastor Anderson who read a draft of the manuscript and said, *"The curse has been broken!"* Amen to that!

About the Author

Early in chiropractic clinical practice, Dr. Patrick Milroy identified his unconscious empathy for people with experiences of assault survivorship. His affinity to help others relates to a repressed sexual assault that took place during his solo bicycle tour in 1986.

Born in St. Paul, Minnesota in 1962, Dr. Milroy holds Bachelor and Masters degrees in Physical Education from the University of Western Ontario. Upon graduation from the Canadian Memorial Chiropractic College in 1994, his personal life and professional career has thrived in Halifax, Nova Scotia.

Whether through writing *The Forest Tabernacle* (his first memoir), or through bicycle touring, chiropractic, or public speaking, Dr. Milroy developed an insatiable passionate for educating on the importance of caring for the temple of the soul – your body, and about the most important journey in life – your spiritual journey and relationship with Jesus.

In clinical practice, his passion and delivery of healing services has helped transform the lives of thousands of people. He continues to reach out to people, groups and organizations to promote recovery from sexual assault and create awareness of issues relating to health. For more information or to schedule Dr. Milroy to speak to your organization, please visit: THEFORESTTABERNACLE.COM.

Speaking

Dr. Milroy is passionate about educating people on the importance of caring for the temple of their souls... the body. His presentations combine scripture with cutting edge knowledge on natural healing and wellness. Dr. Milroy is available to educate audiences within the Sunday service, at conferences and meetings.

Suggested Topics – other topics available by request.

"The Forest Tabernacle: A Healing Journey"
The talk combines reflections and a chapter reading from Dr. Milroy's published memoir, *The Forest Tabernacle: Memoir of Catholicism, Jesus, and a Sexual Assault on a Bicycle Tour.*

"Them Bones of the Bible: A Word about Arthritis"
Basic definitions for OA, RA, DDD, pain and inflammation, role of supplementation, water, sleep, and God's word on healing.

"Cancer? Not in the garden of Eden"
Cellular anti-oxidation through proper dietary and supplementation choices. Explanation regarding God given immortality and disease as a consequence of the fall.

"Christian Men, Grid up Your Loins: Protect Your Prostate"
Reviews early detection. Lifestyle choices for prevention with a special focus on the role of vitamin D and other natural supplements and foods.

"Our Lord's Sweetness"
The perils of high fructose corn syrup (glucose fructose) and the powerful links to diabetes, heart disease and obesity.

"Walk and Pray: Don't Dismay"
The body's stress reaction with focus on the importance of exercise and why walking is so important – even biblical.

"The Living Water"
Physiological importance of water with the message transitioning into Christ, Our Living Water.

"The Godly Vitamin D"
Recent information regarding the role of vitamin D in health. Analogy between light, vitamin D and the 'Light of our Life,' Jesus Christ.

Testimonials for Dr. Patrick Milroy, International Speaker

"Dr. Milroy delivers an engaging presentation that both informs and engages people, giving practical steps for increasing their wellness. People laugh and learn – great medicine in the moment and motivation for healthy futures!"

~ Michael A. Poworoznyk, Former Coordinator of the Cobequid Community Health Board for Capital Health, Nova Scotia

"Dr. Patrick Milroy is a gifted presenter and health practitioner. He has the unique ability to communicate critical and sometimes sensitive material to a wide audience by making real-life comparisons. His learnt expertise and his humble demeanor allow audiences to trust him as he speaks to their physical and spiritual person. Truly, Dr. Milroy is a gifted health practitioner and presenter in the kingdom of God."

~ Pastor Michael Fisher, Executive Pastor, Emmanuel Baptist Church, Upper Hammonds Plains, Nova Scotia

"As a financial planner of 15 years, I wanted a chance to educate my clients about financial health. Speaking to our 200 clients, Dr. Milroy taught them about the relationship between their financial, mental and physical health. His talks are both informative and entertaining."

~ Mr. Michael Nicoletopoulos, Financial Planner, Halifax, Nova Scotia

"I have known Dr. Patrick Milroy for the past six years as a Brother in Christ as well as an outstanding Chiropractor who is a committed Christian. He is a gifted teacher regarding the relationship between the physical health of people and how it relates to the Bible. I recommend him as a person of Christian integrity who could surely benefit the Body of Christ in these days of confusion and great needs in the Church."

~ Rev. Pastor Carl Price, Lower Sackville, Nova Scotia

International Health Publishing

Inspiring readers of the world to experience the light.
International Health Publishing books express truth and wisdom, encourage spiritual enlightenment, facilitate growth and healing – while also providing a phenomenal reading experience.

International Health Publishing's vision is to increase the number and quality of books and resources available to the public, students and Doctors of Chiropractic – allowing for greater understanding, increased education, as well as more visibility and accessibility of the Chiropractic profession as a means of preventative and continued health care.

International Health Publishing
Adjusting and Growing
International Headquarters • Carrollton, Texas
www.InternationalHealthPublishing.com